MUSICAL STRUCTURE AND STYLE

•

an introduction

MUSICAL STRUCTURE AND STYLE

an introduction

CHARLES H. BALL
The University of Tennessee
Knoxville

GENERAL LEARNING PRESS
250 James Street
Morristown, New Jersey 07960

Manufactured in the United States of America.

Published simultaneously in Canada.

Library of Congress Catalog Card Number 74-24464

ISBN 0-382-18052-6

Contents

CONTENTS

Preface

This book exists to provide a concise introduction to the elements and structure of music. Beginning with sound, the basic material of music, it progresses through a study of musical elements, forms, and styles. In so doing, an attempt is made to cover as wide a range of music as is practical without making excessive demands on limited music libraries. The use of notation has been held to a minimum, and in no case is an understanding of notation absolutely essential to an understanding of the text. Similarly, an attempt is made to avoid technical terms, whenever possible, until some basis for their understanding has been established. The concepts discussed here are those underlying most traditional Western music and are applicable to all kinds of music, not the concert repertory alone. The last chapter provides a brief introduction to other musical systems. The author believes this distribution of emphasis to be justified in a book designed as a one-semester text for the general student. It is hoped that by reducing the text to fundamental and widely applicable concepts, the resourceful teacher will be provided maximum flexibility in the presentation of the course. The student will be given access to the most essential information in readily available form, free from unessential embellishment.

The author wishes to express his gratitude to those whose talents and hard work contributed so much to this book: to text designer, Peter Berkeley; to cover designer, Douglas Steinbauer; to music autographer, Maxwell Weaner; and especially to the editor, Wallace W. Schmidt, whose patience and wise guidance made this book both an education and a pleasure to its author.

MUSICAL STRUCTURE AND STYLE
•
an introduction

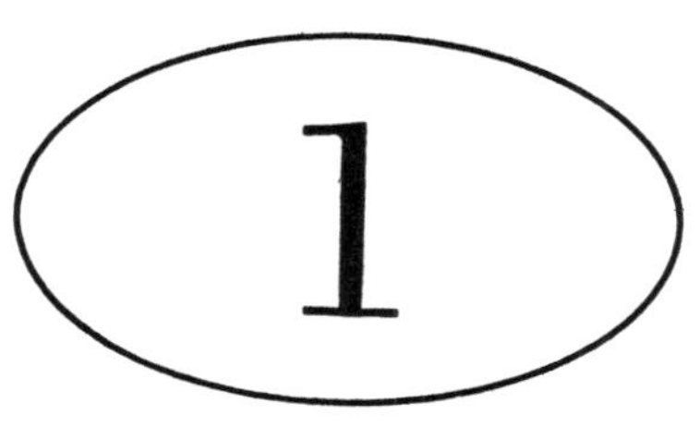

ESSENTIALS OF MUSICAL UNDERSTANDING

THIS

is a book about musical understanding. It is not, strictly speaking, a book about music appreciation. The direct teaching of musical appreciation has some discernible difficulties. It assumes that the teacher has better taste than the student. It further assumes that the teacher has both the moral right and the power to change the student's taste in such manner as to conform to his own. These are very doubtful assumptions, so this book will not mention the subject of taste or appreciation in a direct way. This does not imply a lack of concern for musical taste; it simply means that a different method is employed here.

ESSENTIALS OF MUSICAL UNDERSTANDING

This simple method embodies one idea: If a person can be led to an understanding of music through an exposure to a variety of types and styles of music, he will be able to choose, in a knowledgeable and intellectually honest way, the music which has meaning for him. Accordingly, this book is concerned more directly with understanding than with appreciation. Why should it be necessary to study music in order to understand it? What is there to understand? Music is everywhere: on the radio, on television, on the bus, in the grocery store, in the dentist's office. You cannot escape it. It belongs to everyone. Isn't it overcomplicating the whole thing to say that music must be understood and that this understanding must be learned?

Perhaps the answer can best be made by drawing some analogies between music and other arts, such as drama. Most plays can be understood, on a basic level, without any knowledge of dramatic principles. A story is a story and must be obvious to the audience. But to the playwright it is a different matter. He must make the story come alive for the audience, and he can do so only if he understands dramatic construction. He must know how to make his characters appear to be real people and not just empty shadows. He must know how to produce and resolve conflict. The audience does not have to know any of these things to understand the play on its most basic level. But if the audience does understand these things, a new level of understanding and appreciation is opened. Not only can the story be enjoyed for its most obvious aspects, but it can be understood, and perhaps admired, for its craft and subtlety as well. More important than this, sometimes the actual meaning of the work is embodied not in those surface aspects, but in the subtleties of the dramatic form.

Consider Arthur Miller's *Death of a Salesman*. Willy Loman's tragedy was no more than can be read in any newspaper on any morning. Why is the newspaper account less moving than the play? The answer lies, of course, in the way in which the play is constructed. The flashback technique is employed in such a way that the audience can see, little by little, from the vantage point of the present, the events which have brought Willy to his dilemma. The only thing in doubt is the resolution. Then when it comes, in such a quietly violent manner, the effect is overpowering. The simple graveside speech of the wife seems to sum up all the tragedy which can befall the common man. The power stems entirely from the construction of the play. The effect is, of course, obvious to anyone. But the highest level of understanding and appreciation is open only to the audience fully aware of the ways in which the effect has been achieved.

In the same way a work of music speaks for itself. It is available on some level to anyone who hears. But it gives its meaning fully only to those who understand something of its structural principles. It is not only what is being said that is important, it is also the way in which it is being said. For instance, Shakespeare may have had this thought:

I think all previous literary descriptions
of beautiful people were written by clairvoyants,
who foresaw what you would look like.

But, fortunately, he said it in this way:

SONNET No. 106

When in the chronicle of wasted time
   I see descriptions of the fairest wights,
And beauty making beautiful old rhyme
   In praise of ladies dead and lovely knights,
Then, in the blazon of sweet beauty's best,
   Of hand, of foot, of lip, of eye, of brow,
I see their antique pen would have express'd
   Even such a beauty as you master now.

So all their praises are but prophecies
   Of this our time, all you prefiguring;
And, for they look'd but with divining eyes,
   They had not skill enough your worth to sing:
For we, which now behold these present days,
Have eyes to wonder, but lack tongues to praise.

Undeniably the meaning of that sonnet is a function of its form. The mere sound of the words is a vehicle for the expression of great beauty, but it is the structure that makes the poem what it is. And it is the same with a piece of music.

The surface power of the sound may be intense, but it is the structure which carries the deepest meaning. Such meaning is available only to those who have some understanding of musical structure. To open the doors to such understanding is the purpose of this book.

Just what is there to understand? Before we try to answer that question, perhaps we should attempt a definition of music. We seek one in the sound of music, for example:

MOZART: *Eine kleine Nachtmusik, K.525*, First Movement

As you listen to the music, what do you hear? Of course you hear sounds–sounds of a certain kind, made by certain instruments, and put together to form certain "tunes." These melodies progress through a certain period of time. This time is arranged in certain patterns of rhythm and form. So we might say that music, at least as exemplified by this brief work, might be defined as sounds organized in time. This is, in fact, a common definition of music. But, if you listen and think a bit more, you will discover that this definition leaves out an important feature of the music. For the sounds are put together in such a way that they are not merely arranged or organized in time, but so that each tone seems to give birth to the next; each tone of music seems to move to the next, not just be replaced by it. It is, in fact, this sense of motion which gives the music life. So we might adopt this definition: **Music is sound moving in time.**

Such dictionary definitions are dangerous. They sound very pat, very authoritative, and very final. Of course, nothing is that clear cut, and nothing very profound can be that pat. We shall see that this definition will require alteration when we come to certain examples of twentieth century music. But it is essentially correct and is quite useful, because it embodies most of the essentials of music: **sound**, **time**, and **motion**.

We are speaking now of music of all kinds, styles, types, and categories. Instead of the Mozart example we just heard, we might just as well have used any other piece of music: Beethoven, Basie, or Blood, Sweat and Tears. All music is made of the same elements. We are concerned with those elements and the principles by which they may be combined.

In studying music we must address three main topics: the sound itself, the principles by which sounds are combined, and the variety of results possible from the varied application of these principles. We are concerned with sound, structure, and style. All these will be discussed in detail later in the book, but we should talk about them now, in a preliminary way, to be certain we understand just what we are about.

Sound is such an obvious thing that we need not concern ourselves with it in great detail at this early point. Structure and style, however, are more subtle topics. In order to understand these ideas better, we must turn to some definitions and examples. By structure we mean, simply, the manner in which a piece is organized. The elemental sounds must be deployed in some way, according to some principles, in order to produce a piece of music. The result is structure. Structure is common to all kinds, types, and styles of music. Whether we write a symphony or a popular song, a folk song or a march, the basic structural principles are the same. However, the particular ways in which the structure is achieved and the particular results may vary widely in specific instances. A symphony differs from a folk song, a popular song, or a march; each of these types of composition may also vary with others of the same type. It is the manner in which a composer achieves structure that determines the particular musical style.

An analogy might be helpful at this point. Consider this poem by Robert Herrick:

UPON JULIA'S CLOTHES

Whenas in silks my Julia goes,
Then, then, methinks, how sweetly flows
The liquefaction of her clothes.

Next, when I cast mine eyes, and see
That brave vibration, each way free,
Oh, how that glittering taketh me.

The poet set out with an idea. He began with an infinity of possible ways in which to express it. This is the one he finally worked out. We can describe the structure of the poem easily. We can point out that the poem consists of two stanzas of three lines each. We note that each line is made up of four rhythmic groups, each consisting of an unstressed and a stressed syllable. We may say further that the final word of each of the three lines rhymes with the other finals of that stanza. Having done this, we have fairly well described the structure of the poem. It is important to note that such an analysis says nothing about the effect of the poem, but only about the structural features which influence it. It does not change a thing about the poem. It simply helps us understand it. It does this in two ways. First, it sharpens our awareness of the poetic process. Second, it causes us to pay closer attention to the poem and to participate in it, rather than receiving it passively. This will also be our purpose in analyzing music. It will help us participate, along with the composer and the performer, in a musical event.

To give a brief illustration of what we mean by style, we turn to another example. In this poem Wordsworth is treating a subject similar to the one just examined:

THE PERFECT WOMAN

She was a Phantom of delight
   When first she gleamed upon my sight;
A lovely apparition, sent
   To be a moment's ornament;

Her eyes as stars of Twilight Fair;
Like Twilight's, too, her dusky hair;
But all things else about her drawn
From May-time and the cheerful Dawn;
A dancing Shape, an Image gay,
To haunt, to startle, and way-lay.

I saw her upon nearer view,
A spirit, yet a Woman too;
Her household motions light and free,
And steps of virgin-liberty;
A countenance in which did meet
Sweet records, promises as sweet;
A Creature not too bright or good
For human nature's daily food;
For transient sorrows, simple wiles,
Praise, blame, love, kisses, tears, and smiles.

And now I see with eye serene
The very pulse of the machine;
A Being breathing thoughtful breath,
A Traveller between life and death;
The reason firm, the temperate will,
Endurance, foresight, strength, and skill;
A perfect Woman, nobly planned,
To warm, to comfort, and command;
And yet a Spirit still, and bright
With something of angelic light.

We could analyze this poem structurally in the same way we did the previous one. Except for the greater length of this example, the structural differences would not be great. But still, the over all difference in the poems is striking. These are differences of style. Herrick's language is simple, while Wordsworth's is elaborate. Herrick selected one image; Wordsworth painted a series of images. Herrick used words in a straightforward manner; Wordsworth laced his poem with metaphors.

This should be enough to illustrate what we mean by stylistic differences. It should serve also to illustrate that style involves structure, but transcends it. While style must be related intimately to structure, it involves elements and usages other than purely structural ones. This is true, also, of music. Just as we have analyzed the structure of a poem, we may analyze the structure of a musical composition. Just as different linguistic usages result in different poetic styles, different usages of sound result in different musical styles, and these are subject to analysis.

This musical analysis, though, contains some difficulties not encountered in the analysis of poetry. We have all studied language throughout our school days. We have had some contact with poetry. But we have not, as a rule, had an opportunity to learn the grammar of music, nor to become familiar with the artistic ends to which this grammar may be put. This book exists to provide that opportunity. Just as we deal with words combined into poetic feet and lines, we must learn to deal with tones combined into metrical groupings, phrases, and melodies. Just as sentences portray images, we must see that melodies carry musical ideas. Just as stanzas are formed from lines, and in turn form larger sections and parts of a poem, we must see that musical phrases combine into sections, sections into larger sections, these larger sections into movements, and movements into symphonies. Most important of all, we must realize that just as the structure and shape of a poem result in the expression of poetic effects, the structure and shape of a piece of music carry musical meaning—meaning not definable in words, but meaning nevertheless.

Our course is clear, then. First, we must explore the nature of sound itself. This must lead to a study of the elements of music: rhythm, melody, and harmony. Then we must see how these elements combine into musical forms. Finally, we must use this knowledge to help us become sensitive to musical styles. This is the plan which the book will follow. At each stage, we shall try to learn from actual musical examples. It is important to remember that we are only learning the rules of musical grammar from this book, and we are learning it only as a tool. The book can only help open our ears; the music then can speak for itself.

SOUND: THE BASIC MATERIAL OF MUSIC

14
MUSICAL STRUCTURE AND STYLE

WE *have defined music as sound moving in time. We have seen how organized sound in motion produces structure. We have also noted that the particular manner in which the sound moves constitutes style. Understanding music is, largely, understanding structure and style. But before these can be studied, we must address ourselves to a brief consideration of the raw material of music—sound itself. Therefore, we shall briefly investigate several aspects of sound, including both its physical bases and its aesthetic effects.*

THE PHYSICAL BASES OF SOUND

*

All sound is produced by some vibrating body. Suppose, for example, a tuning fork is struck. It will vibrate, and these vibrations will, in turn, set into motion the air surrounding the fork. This results in the alternate compression and rarefaction of the molecules of the air, producing a sound wave. If this wave were pictured on an oscilloscope, it would look something like Example 2.1.

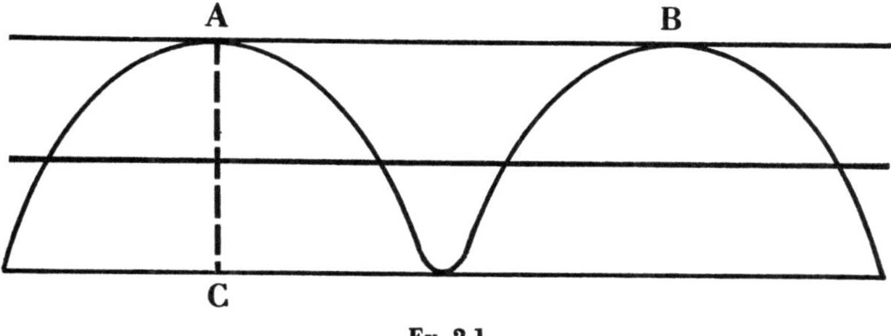

Ex. 2.1

By examining this pictorial representation of a sound wave, we can learn several things about the nature of sound. First we notice that the wave is regular in shape. The crests and troughs of the wave occur in a regular, measurable pattern. This is important, because it is this regularity and measurability that account for some of the musical qualities of sound which make it useful for artistic purposes.

Consider the length of the wave. The distance from one crest to the next, from A to B in the diagram, is called the wave length. This is directly related to the frequency of the waves produced by the vibrating body. The physical characteristics of the tuning fork determine the rate at which it will vibrate and dictate the length of the wave. The faster the rate of vibration, the shorter will be the wave length. This is perceived by the ear as pitch. The faster the rate of vibration, the higher the pitch sounds to the ear. This characteristic of sound is probably the most important one for the art of music, because the tonal, or pitch-related, organization of sound is the most basic aspect of music.

Now let us look at the depth of the wave, represented in the diagram by the distance from A to C. Any wave, regardless of the wave length, may be of any depth. This is a function, in the case of the tuning fork, of the distance travelled by the fork during its vibrations; the farther the fork travels, the deeper will be the wave. This difference in depth, or amplitude, of various waves is experienced by the ear as a difference of loudness. The deeper the wave, the louder the tone will sound. Although this is simpler than the subject of pitch, it is important to music, for the ability to vary loudness is a vital part of musical expression.

To this point we have been considering a simple type of sound wave produced by a simple type of vibrating body. In reality such a sound wave is seldom encountered. Most wave forms are more complex and are more difficult to describe and measure. Let us suppose that we have a violin or a guitar for our use. When a string is plucked it will vibrate at a frequency dependent upon its physical characteristics—its length, diameter, and tension. It will vibrate not only along its entire length, but also in segments. Each of two halves of the string will vibrate, four fourths will vibrate, and so on. Each of these vibrating segments will produce its own wave, with all the characteristics we have seen above. The additional tones thus produced are called overtones. If we could view this on the oscilloscope, we would find that all these various waves are superimposed upon each other, producing what appears to be one complex waveform. To the ear this waveform is heard not as a group of superimposed pitches, but as a certain tone quality or timbre.

Different types of vibrating bodies produce the various overtones in different combinations and in different amplitudes. The particular combination of overtones, and the various amplitudes of these overtones, produce different timbres. Some instruments produce few overtones, and the result is a simple waveform with its attendant pure, flute-like quality. Other instruments, such as the oboe or the violin, produce many overtones and give a much richer tone color.

These characteristics of the sound wave—frequency, amplitude, and wave form—are of fundamental importance to the art of music. The corresponding subjective qualities of tone—**pitch**, **intensity**, and **timbre**—are the essence from which the composer fashions his work. One other characteristic of sound should be mentioned, even though it is not, strictly speaking, a quality of sound. That is **duration**. If a sound exists, it exists for a specific length of time. This is important to the composer. We shall see this to be true in a variety of ways when we discuss rhythm. These characteristics of sound can be pictured as follows:

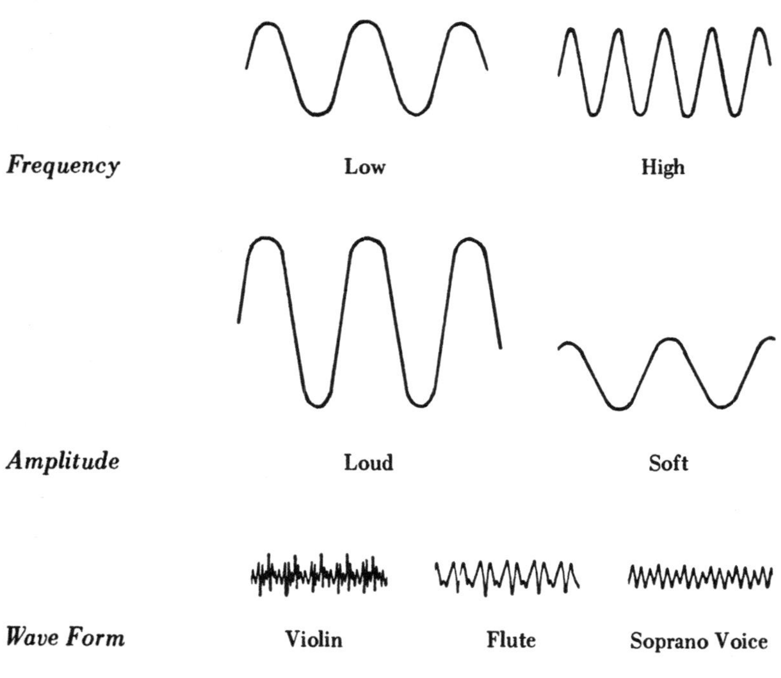

Ex. 2.2

THE MUSICAL USES OF SOUND

*

At this point we will turn to some musical examples of how sound can be put to artistic uses. Even though the composer can vary sound in only a limited number of basic ways, an almost limitless variety of artistic results can be achieved. For a starting point, let us listen to a musical composition and see what can be said about the sound:

BACH: *Brandenburg Concerto No. 3*, First Movement

Using what we know about the basic characteristics of sound, plus a little common sense, we can give a rough description of the effect of the composition. First, we can say, in regard to pitch, that a fairly wide range is covered, but that the median pitch, or **tessitura**, is relatively low. Concerning loudness, the composition is moderate, neither very loud nor very soft, and displays little variety in levels of loudness. The timbre is uniform and variety of tone color plays no part in the composition. The music is made up of short tones moving at a fairly rapid pace and the over all effect is one of vigorous activity. This can hardly be called a detailed technical analysis, but it is at least descriptive of the most elementary aspects of the sound. For contrast we hear a second example:

HINDEMITH: *Morgenmusik for Brass*, First Section

This is a very different sound from the previous example. The pitch range covered is also fairly wide, but the tessitura is somewhat higher than in the previous composition. While the loudness range is limited to practically no variety, the overall loudness is a little greater. Again, the timbre is uniform, but the timbre of this example is very different from that in the *Brandenburg Concerto*. The duration of tones in this piece are longer and move at a slower pace. Finally, the overall impression is more majestic in nature, with less vigor and agitation of movement. These contrasts show us some of the differences which can result from the manipulation of the basic characteristics of sound. To develop the point further, we turn to a third example:

STRAUSS: *Also sprach Zarathustra*, Opening Fanfare

Here is a really different sound. The pitch range of this composition is immense, from the initial low growling bass tone to the highest tones at the end of the fanfare. This time the loudness range is also great, from the softest tones imaginable to the great crashing climax. It should be noted that this loudness range is used purposefully, building slowly from soft to loud and thus intensifying the gradual growth leading to the climax of the fanfare. The timbre is not uniform, but contains great variety. The duration of the tones is moderate, for the most part, and the piece moves at a moderate pace. Despite the simplicity of this account of the pace of the composition, this is important because this pacing intensifies the slow growth which characterizes the fanfare. Each tone seems loath to move ahead to the next, almost as if some inertia were preventing the forward motion. The net effect is one of increasing intensity.

These analyses are only roughly descriptive, but they provide a beginning for the kind of description necessary to the understanding of music. We must be able to describe what is heard before we can hope to understand what aesthetic purpose is being served by what we hear. In the Strauss composition, the slow, labored movement from tone to tone has to be described before its aesthetic purpose—the building toward a climax—can be understood.

As you listened to these examples, the most striking differences noted in the sound of the various pieces were differences of timbre. This is, probably, the most easily discerned quality of musical sound. The timbre of the different compositions was determined by the particular combinations of instruments used. If we are to be able to exercise intelligent listening habits, we must be familiar with musical instruments. For this reason we turn our attention to a brief description of the most widely used instruments. The most important thing we can learn about them is the variety of actual sounds they produce. For this reason, we should listen to a variety of recorded and live examples. The ability to recognize the several instruments is indispensable to anyone who wishes to become a skilled listener.

INSTRUMENTS OF THE ORCHESTRA

❀

It might seem strange that we choose to classify instruments into the categories of orchestral and non-orchestral. The reason is that the greatest body of enduring music, with the exception of that written for the piano, has been written for the orchestra and for certain smaller combinations of instruments drawn from the orchestra.

The orchestra consists of four sections, or choirs, classified by the manner in which the instruments produce sound. We have seen that all sound is produced by a vibrating body. This body may be one of several kinds. It may be a vibrating membrane, a string, or simply a column of air. In the latter case, the air may be set into motion by a reed or by the lips of the player. The orchestra contains instruments using each of these methods of tone production.

The four choirs or sections of the orchestra are string, woodwind, brass, and percussion. Some instruments, such as the harp and the celesta, do not fall conveniently into one or the other of these categories, but for the most part these classifications serve their descriptive purposes. The string section consists of those instruments which produce tone by setting a string into motion by the drawing of a bow. The woodwind family contains three classes of instruments: those employing the same principle used when sound is produced from an empty bottle, those using a single reed, and those using a double reed. The brass instruments produce sound by using the vibrating lips of the player to set in motion a column of air within the instrument. The percussion section includes those instruments that are struck or beaten either with the hand or with a stick or mallet. You will hear each of these sections performing separately and as a full orchestra in the following musical example:

BRITTEN: *Variations on a Theme of Purcell*, Statement

The String Choir

*

BARBER: *Adagio for Strings*

VAUGHAN WILLIAMS: *Fantasia on a Theme of Thomas Tallis*

The string family consists of four instruments: the **violin**, the **viola**, the **violoncello**, and the **string bass**. The violin is the most familiar of these and is the highest pitched member of the group. The viola is pitched five tones lower than the violin. The viola differs from the violin not only in size and tuning, but also in tone quality. It has a darker tone quality which is distinctive and has great expressive possibilities. The violoncello, commonly called the cello, is so large that it must rest with one end on the floor, and the bow is drawn horizontally. It sounds an octave lower than the viola. The cello is widely used in solo passages. The largest member of the string family is the string bass.

The string choir covers an immense pitch range. It is also capable to playing in a wide dynamic range from a whisper of sound to an overpowering loudness. In matters of execution, the strings can play from the fastest and most florid passages to the most sustained lyric sections. But perhaps most important of all are the expressive possibilities which the strings offer.

These instruments are played by drawing a bow across the strings. However, the bow may be drawn in a nearly endless variety of ways, and each manner of drawing the bow produces a different effect, with different expressive possibilities. For instance, the bow may be used in its entirety, it may be drawn only at the tip, or it may be drawn only at the frog (the end of the bow nearest the hand). A different effect is produced in each of these three cases. The bow may be drawn lightly or with its full weight on the string. It may be played with the bow always contacting the string, or the bow may be bounced. The bow may be moved rapidly back and forth across the string, producing a *tremolo*. It may be turned over so that the strings are struck by the wood part of the bow, producing an effect called *col legno*. The bow may be abandoned entirely and the strings plucked with the fingers, a technique known as *pizzicato*.

In addition to these effects, two other special tonal possibilities of the strings should be mentioned. The first of these is the use of the mute, a small wooden or rubber device used to damp the vibrations of the instrument and dull the tone. The other is the use of harmonics. By lightly touching the string with a finger while the bow is in motion, the string may be made to produce only one of the upper overtones, rather than the fundamental pitch. This tone is not only higher in pitch, but is thinner and lighter in timbre.

The Woodwind Choir

*

MOZART: *Serenade in E-flat, Woodwinds, K.375*

The woodwind instruments produce sounds by means of a vibrating column of air. The different means of setting this air into motion produce a heterogeneous sound within the woodwind choir, in contrast to the homogeneity of the strings. This heterogeneity results in less perfect blend within the section, but makes possible a great variety of tone colors, especially useful for solo passages.

In discussing the woodwinds we shall first consider the **flute**, on which sound is produced by blowing across an open hole. The flute is capable of executing very rapid scale passages throughout its entire range. In addition to its extreme agility, it is capable of producing very different effects in different pitch ranges, or registers. The flute has two very close relatives which are also important to the orchestra: the **piccolo** and the **alto flute.** The piccolo is a small flute which produces a high and a piercing sound. The alto flute is larger and has a warm, velvety quality similar to the flute's lower range.

The orchestral instruments producing their tones by means of a single reed are the **clarinet** and the **bass clarinet.** The clarinet has a very wide range and produces a variety of tone qualities. The highest and lowest registers are distinctive in quality. The clarion register is brilliant and penetrating while the chalumeau register is rich and dark. The bass clarinet has a full and mellow sound similar to the chalumeau register of the clarinet. It is seldom used for solo passages, but is important as a bass instrument within the woodwind choir.

The double reed instruments are the **oboe**, the **English horn**, the **bassoon**, and the **contrabassoon**. The oboe is one of the most important solo instruments of the orchestra. In its higher register, the oboe has a plaintive, pastoral quality. The lowest few tones are harsh and penetrating. The English horn is similar in construction, but sounds five tones lower. The English horn has neither the cutting tone of the oboe's upper register nor the harshness of the lower. Its tone is a reedy nasality peculiar to itself. The bass instrument of the double reed family is the bassoon. In the lower register, the gruff tone quality lends itself to frequent use in passages intended to be humorous. In its upper register, the tone is smooth and expressive. The lowest instrument of the double reeds is the contrabassoon. It is used primarily to give power to the bottom of the woodwind section.

The Brass Choir

*

HINDEMITH: *Morgenmusik for Brass*

The brasses are constructed and played in quite a different fashion from the woodwinds. The vibrating body which supplies the sound is the player's own lips, which vibrate within a cup or cone shaped mouthpiece at one end of the long metal tube which is the instrument. By adjusting his lips, the player can sound several different pitches using the same length of tubing. In order to achieve the full musical scale, however, several different lengths of tubing must be employed. To make this possible, the brass instruments use two basic designs. In one, extra lengths of tubing are added by means of valves. In the other, the length of the basic tube can be varied by means of a slide.

The smallest and highest member of the brass family is the **trumpet**. It has a wide dynamic range and is capable of great power, especially in the upper range. It is useful for solo work, as well as in combination with other brass instruments.

The **horn** is a long piece of tubing coiled into a circular shape. Like the trumpet, it has three valves. Its tone blends well with practically every instrument of the orchestra and is extremely valuable in ensemble passages. However, it is also one of the most widely used solo instruments.

The **trombone** slide provides an infinite number of tube lengths within the maximum and minimum lengths available. This gives the player the opportunity to slide, or *glissando*, from note to note, an effect not possible on the other brass instruments. The trombone has a regal and majestic quality. When employed in groups of three or four, trombones can produce a sound of almost overwhelming power.

The bass instruments of the brass family are the **bass trombone** and the **tuba**. The bass trombone is simply a larger and longer version of the trombone. The tuba is larger and is equipped with either three or four valves. It is an instrument of power and beauty, but is also capable of playing very soft and mellow tones. Its great asset is the ability to provide a solid and robust bottom to the sound of the brass choir.

The Percussion Instruments

*

COPLAND: *El Salon Mexico*

The percussion instruments are played by striking with sticks, mallets, or in some cases with the hand. There are so many that a complete listing is hardly practical, so we shall restrict our discussion to those most commonly used. They may be roughly divided into three categories: the drums, the mallet instruments, and the traps, the latter usually being for the purpose of some distinctive type of sound effect. As we shall see, these are the salt and pepper of orchestral music, often not being very noticeable in their presence, but being so important that their absence would stand out conspicuously.

The drums may be divided into two categories, those of indefinite pitch and those of definite pitch. Chief among the former are the **snare drum** and the **bass drum**. The snare drum is familiar to almost everyone from its use in military bands and popular dance combos. Snare drums are characterized by small wires, called snares, which are stretched across the bottom head. These cause the instrument to produce a crisp and incisive sound. The snares may be loosened to produce muffled sound. The bass drum provides punctuation of a different kind. It does not produce quite the incisive quality of the snare drum, but provides a resonant, deep tone. Like the snare drum, the bass drum may be muffled. The **tympani**, or kettle drums have a definite pitch. The tympani exist in various sizes, each of which may be tuned to a narrow range of pitches by the use of a foot pedal.

The mallet instruments are all of definite pitch. They include the **xylophone**, the **marimba**, the **glockenspiel**, the **chimes** and the **vibraphone**. All except the chimes consist of a number of horizontally mounted bars. These are made of wood on the xylophone and marimba and of metal on the glockenspiel and the vibraphone. The vibraphone has a tubular resonator for each bar. In each resonator is a rotating valve which produces a shimmering, tremolo effect. The chimes consist of vertically mounted brass tubes which are struck with a hammer.

All percussion instruments other than drums and mallet instruments may be classified as traps. Among these are the **Chinese gong**, the **castanets**, **cymbals**, **wood block**, **triangle**, **Chinese temple blocks**, and the **whip**. The list could go on and on, but these are some of the most commonly found traps. Most have names descriptive of the sounds they make.

Other Orchestral Instruments

*

TCHAIKOVSKY: *Nutcracker Suite*, The Sugar Plum Fairy

The **celesta** is a small keyboard instrument which produces its tones by the action of hammers upon small steel bars equipped with individual wooden resonators, which produce a sweet and full sound. The celesta is usually considered to be part of the percussion group, but its character and usage is distinctive for coloristic purposes and it has been widely used in impressionistic and descriptive music.

FRANCK: *Symphony in D Minor*, Second Movement

The **harp** does not fit well into any of the categories which we have discussed. It certainly has strings, but it is not played with a bow and bears little resemblance to the other stringed instruments. The harp has many strings, tuned in such a way that broken chords, or *arpeggios*, may be easily played by sweeping the strings with the fingers. The harp has seven pedals which are used to change the pitch of the strings. Through a combination of string selection and pedal usage, the player can produce all the pitches of the chromatic scale.

Non-Orchestral Instruments

*

CRESTON: *Sonata for Saxophone and Piano*

The **saxophones**, although occasionally used in orchestral music, are not considered as standard orchestral instruments. They have achieved a place of importance, however, in the field of popular music and jazz. In addition, some concert music has been written for solo saxophone and for various combinations of saxophones. The saxophones exist in several sizes and pitch ranges: the soprano, alto, tenor, baritone, and bass. The alto and tenor saxes are the most commonly used. The saxophones are conical tubes made of brass and played by a single reed, similar to that of the clarinet. This places them in the woodwind family, even though they are metal.

BACH: *Wachet auf*, Chorale Prelude

The **organ** is one of the oldest and most complex instruments known. An organ could be constructed with only one set of pipes, one for each pitch. A large organ has many sets, or ranks, of pipes, with each rank producing a complete set of pitches of a particular timbre. The flue pipes are similar in construction to a simple whistle, and produce the sound by passing air through a lip, or fipple. The reed pipes produce the sound by passing air through a reed which is mounted in the lip of the pipe. The pipes produce four basic qualities of tone: diapason, which is the characteristic tone of the organ; flute, which is imitative of various types of orchestral flutes and recorders; string, which bears only a very superficial resemblance to the sound of orchestral strings; and reed, which gives power and majesty to the tone. This vast array of pipes is controlled from a console which has keyboards and also a pedal clavier which is played with the feet. In modern times, various attempts to reproduce the sound of the organ in electronic instruments have been made with varying degrees of success.

RODRIGO: *Concierto de Aranjuez*

The **guitar** has gained great popularity in recent years both as an accompanying instrument and for serious solo work. Guitars are of several different types. The classic guitar is an instrument with nylon strings, a wooden body, and a round sound hole. This type of guitar is always plucked with the fingers, rather than with a pick. It is much used in accompanying folk singing and in performing the wealth of solo literature. The folk guitar is similar to the classic guitar, but usually has a larger body and always has steel strings.

Some models are double strung, having twelve strings rather than the customary six. A familiar guitar to contemporary ears is the electric guitar. It may have either a hollow or solid body. Its steel strings produce tones which are amplified electrically and reproduced through a loudspeaker. This has allowed modern players, particularly rock guitarists, to invent some ingenious devices for modifying the sound of the guitar. These include the fuzz box, the tremolo, the wah-wah, and various types of reverberation units.

BYRD: *Pavana: The Earl of Salisbury*

The **harpsichord**, a forerunner of the piano, has strings that are plucked by quills rather than struck by hammers. It has one, and sometimes two, keyboards similar to those of the piano. On larger harpsichords a system of couplers allows several sets of strings to be played at one time. The instrument has a delicate sound, but can gain in power when couplers are employed. The harpsichord has enjoyed a great renaissance in recent years, and many skilled harpsichordists appear in concerts and serve on faculties of music schools and conservatories.

CARLOS: *Switched-On Bach*

SUBOTNICK: *Silver Apples of the Moon*

The **synthesizers** are being modified and reinvented at such a rate that only the briefest account of them can be given here. Operated electronically, the synthesizers aim at virtually complete control over the tonal materials of music. They employ oscillators, filters, envelope generators, and other such devices to provide a staggering range of tonal possibilities. Theoretically, the synthesizer allows the player to produce a tone of any timbre or waveform and to present it with any conceivable type of attack and release. These instruments have become important to modern composers of electronic music, and have also provided a new medium for the performance of other, more traditional music.

This has been a necessarily brief introduction to some of the tonal colors available to the composer. No words can convey the most important aspect of musical instruments—their sound. This can only be done by listening to actual performances.

3

MEDIA FOR MUSICAL PERFORMANCE

WE

have been introduced to the sounds of many of the more important musical instruments. Before moving ahead to a study of the elements of music, we should consider briefly some of the ways these instruments are used to influence the sound of music. This, in turn, will lead us to an introduction to several performing media which have become historically important.

TONE COLOR AND ITS INFLUENCE ON MUSIC

*

Tone color is so important to the sound of any composition that it is sometimes treated as one of the elements of music. We have heard the sounds of many solo instruments and of the four instrumental families. We have yet to hear the great varieties of tone color which the almost endless available combinations of instruments can yield. Before we do so, let us hear and compare two recorded performances of the same piece as an illustration of the powerful influence of tone color upon musical effect.

MUSSORGSKY: *Pictures at an Exhibition*, Gate at Kiev

This suite was first written for piano solo and then orchestrated by Ravel at a later time. The tones are the same in both versions; the effects are very different. Each performance has its own character and, in a way, its own type of appeal. The monochromatic rendering of the piano solo is completely different from the spectacular and brilliantly colorful orchestrated version. You may take your choice, but you could never confuse the two. This illustrates, in a somewhat extreme way, the profound influence of tone color upon the aesthetic effect of music.

The degree of importance tone color is accorded varies from

piece to piece and from composer to composer. Obviously a composition intended for a solo instrument is not capable of being influenced by tone color so much as one written for orchestra or band. Less obviously, a composition by Mozart emphasizes color less than one by Debussy or Ravel. The use of tone color is an important element in a composer's style. This is something we shall have occasion to discuss at length later in the book. But for now we may at least hear a few examples illustrating differences in the use of tone color.

MOZART: *Symphony No. 40 in G Minor*, Third Movement

BEETHOVEN: *Symphony No. 3, Opus 55*, Third Movement

TCHAIKOVSKY: *Symphony No. 6, Opus 74*, Fourth Movement

RAVEL: *Daphnis et Chloé*, Suite No. 2

STRAVINSKY: *Petrouchka*, Ballet Suite

These pieces are listed in order of increasing coloristic importance. The Mozart symphony depends little upon tone color for its effect, the Beethoven symphony only a bit more. To Tchaikovsky, the color is important to a high degree, to Ravel more yet, and to Stravinsky it is absolutely vital. This is enough to illustrate stylistic differences in the use of tone color and to indicate the great differences attributable to different uses and combinations of instruments.

The desire to fit together the best combinations of tone

colors for particular compositions, together with many practical considerations of performance, has resulted in a variety of traditional performing media. A complete catalogue of these is impossible because of the almost infinite number of such media. Neither is it possible to engage in a comprehensive and exhaustive discussion of any one of them. But we can briefly consider those which history has demonstrated to be most important, and we can listen to examples of each.

The Orchestra

*

There is little doubt that the symphony orchestra is the most important performing medium history has thus far given us. The great body of orchestral literature attests to this. The reason is easy to understand: The orchestra offers the greatest variety of color and the greatest range of expressive possibilities of any performing medium. This is true because it includes instruments of all the basic families, unlike the band which does not contain strings. In addition, the instrumentation of an orchestra makes possible a great range of dynamics. It can play from the softest tone of a single flute to the loudest sound of the full orchestra. And that is a loud sound indeed because of the great size of the ensemble.

Although the exact instrumentation of the orchestra may vary slightly according to the work being performed, the typical modern orchestra will have sixteen or eighteen first violins, approximately the same number of second violins, twelve violas, twelve cellos, nine or ten string basses, three flutes, piccolo, three oboes, English horn, three or four clarinets, three bassoons, contrabassoon, four to six horns, three or four trumpets, three or four trombones, tuba, one or two harps, and percussion. A typical arrangement might look like this:

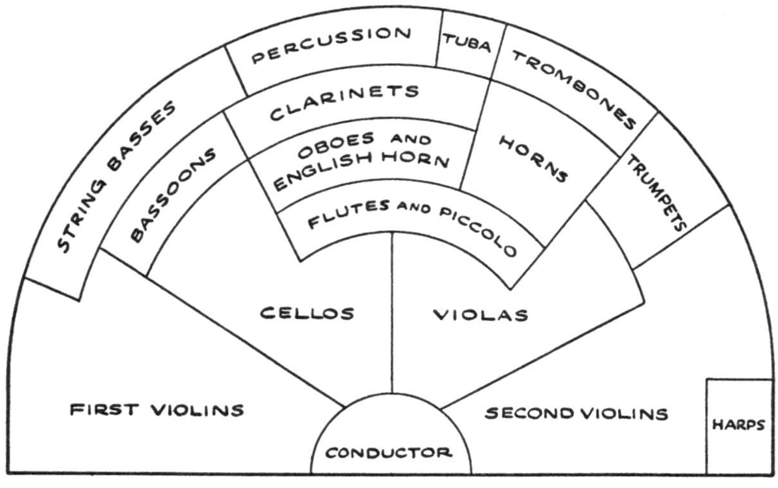

Ex. 3.1

Some suggestions for listening are:

BEETHOVEN: *Symphony No. 6, Opus 68, Pastoral*

WAGNER: *Seigfried Idyll*

RAVEL: *Daphnis et Chloé*, Suite No. 2

The Band

*

The instrumentation of the band is not standardized to the same extent as that of the orchestra. The basic characteristics of the band are the same, however, regardless of the exact complement of instruments. It differs from the orchestra in that the band contains no string instruments, except for an occasional string bass in the symphonic band. The basic sound of the traditional band is that of the clarinets, just as the basic sound of the orchestra is that of the strings. The band contains many important wind instruments not found in the orchestra, such as the contrabass clarinet, the euphonium, and the saxophone. A smaller group, called the wind ensemble, with only one player for each line of music, has become an important variation of the basic band. A characteristic concert band might be arranged this way:

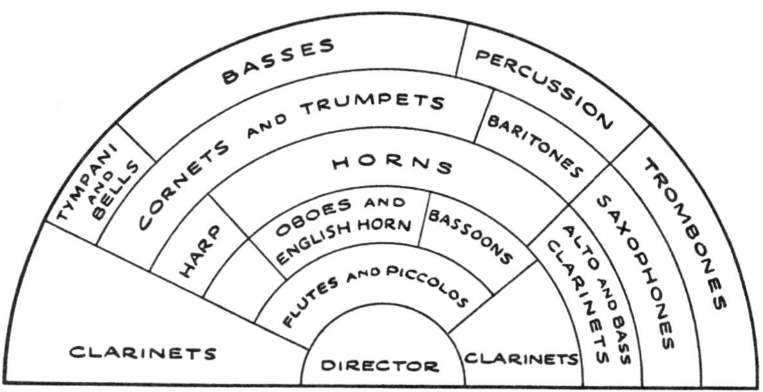

Ex. 3.2

Although band literature at one time was limited to marches and orchestral transcriptions, the situation is now very different. Many composers have become interested in the possibilities inherent in the sound of the band and have produced a great number of excellent compositions. Given this interest and the high level of involvement in school and college bands, there may develop a large and significant body of literature for the band. Some typical compositions are:

SOUSA: *El Capitan*

HOLST: *Suite No. 1 for Band*

Chamber Music

*

Chamber music is intended to be performed in small rooms. The variety of ensembles which have evolved for the performance of chamber music is practically unlimited. These consist of trios, quartets, quintets, sextets, septets, octets, and practically every other conceivable type of ensemble containing every imaginable combination of instruments. Without question the most important of the traditional chamber ensembles is the string quartet. It consists of first and second violins, viola, and cello. Most of the major composers of the past two hundred years have written for this ensemble, and many professional quartets are active on the concert stage today.

Besides the string quartet, a bewildering variety of chamber ensembles may be found. Among these are the woodwind quintet, consisting of flute, clarinet, oboe, horn, and bassoon; the brass quintet, consisting of two trumpets, horn, trombone, and tuba; and various combinations of strings with solo instrument. Some typical examples are:

String Quartet

BRAHMS: *Quartet No. 1, Opus 51, No. 1*

BORODIN: *Quartet No. 2 in D*

BARTÓK: *Quartet No. 1*

Woodwind Quintet

HINDEMITH: *Kleine Kammermusik, Opus 24, No. 2*

Brass Quintet

GABRIELI: *Sonata Pian' e Forte*

Clarinet and Strings

MOZART: *Quintet in A, K.581*

Varied Instrumental Ensembles

BEETHOVEN: *Octet in E-flat for Winds, Opus 103*

STRAVINSKY: *Histoire du Soldat*

Solo Instruments

*

In any discussion of performing media, the importance of solo instruments should not be overlooked. The piano and the organ are particularly important solo instruments because of their self-sufficiency. The violin, the cello, and to a lesser extent, some of the wind instruments are also important as solo media, although these instruments usually are accompanied by the piano. In addition to the music for solo instruments and for solo instruments and piano, there exists a vast literature for solo instruments and orchestra. We shall have occasion to discuss this in detail when we study the concerto. As examples of music for solo instruments and for solo instruments with piano or orchestra, the following are typical:

CHOPIN: *Fantasy in F Minor, Opus 49,* Solo Piano

BACH: *Suite No. 3 in C*, Solo Cello

DEBUSSY: *Syrinx*, Solo Flute

BERKELEY: *Sonatina, Opus 51*, Solo Guitar

IBERT: *Concertino da Camera*, Saxophone and Orchestra

BEETHOVEN: *Sonata No. 9, Opus 47*, Violin and Piano

MOZART: *Concerto in B-flat, K.191*, Bassoon and Orchestra

RODRIGO: *Concierto de Aranjuez*, Guitar and Orchestra

Voices

*

The voice as an instrument has not been mentioned thus far in our discussion. But it is in every sense one of major importance. Vocal music exists in every medium from the solo song, through various chamber music compositions, to music for large chorus. Voices are classified according to range and tone quality. Women's voices, beginning with the highest pitched, are soprano, mezzo-soprano, and contralto. Men's voices are tenor, baritone, and bass. Many variations in the particular character of these voices account for such classifications as bass-baritone, coloratura soprano, dramatic soprano, and many others. Still, all are varieties of the six basic voice types.

The number and variety of vocal ensembles is staggering. Most are built around four vocal parts: soprano, alto, tenor, and bass. The actual performing groups may contain as few as four voices—one per line—or as many as two or three hundred in the largest choruses. We shall have occasion to sample many of these later in our study. Some compositions for vocal ensembles are:

BERLIOZ: *Requiem*

PALESTRINA: *Missa Papae Marcelli*

BRAHMS: *Liebeslieder Waltzes, Opus 52 and Opus 65*

This brief introduction can do little more than make us aware of the importance of performing media. As with everything in music, the importance lies not in discussing these media but in listening to them.

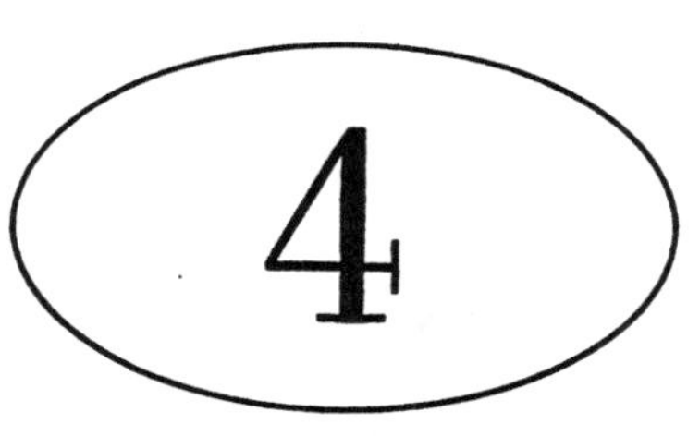

RHYTHM: THE TEMPORAL ORGANIZATION OF MUSIC

RHYTHM,

the most basic, and possibly the most important of the musical elements, is often defined as the temporal aspect of music. There is a danger inherent in dictionary definitions, and we shall see that rhythm consists of much more than this simple definition implies. Music is *a temporal art. What is the composer trying to do with time when he writes a piece of music? How are the elements of music deployed in time to result in a coherent and expressive composition? How are the temporal aspects of tone made understandable to the listener? These are questions basic to the art of music and to our understanding of music.*

Time is what music is all about. Without the passage of time, sound could serve no artistic purpose. It is the deployment of that sound in time that constitutes a piece of music. The composer arranges sound in such a manner that it forms a coherent structure. That structure depends upon time. The temporal relationships between the tonal components of a piece constitute the form of the piece, and, therefore, the piece itself. In a real sense, the composer is creating a temporal illusion—an illusion of tonal motion through time. To do this, he must have some way of measuring the duration of the tones. He must be able to apportion various time values to the tones in such a way that the result makes sense to the listener. Our study of rhythm embraces two aspects. The first is the simple measurement of tones. The second is the employment of this measurement to produce musical meaning.

THE THREE LEVELS OF RHYTHMIC ORGANIZATION

The Beat

How can each tone of a composition be measured and given its proper place? What units of measurement can be employed? Since time has been successfully measured by the clock, music should be measurable in the same way. Tones should be capable of measurement in seconds, multiples of a second, or fractions of a second. This is done in many twentieth century compositions, but this method has difficulties. For one thing, it is very difficult to attain accurate measurements of very short tones. Another is the nature of clock time and its relation to the time contained within a musical composition. In making the temporal illusion that we call music, a composer is less concerned with absolute time than he is with creating his own special slice of self contained, illusory time. To do this, he must produce the illusion of motion. His measurement of time must be accomplished in some way which is related to this sense of motion, and, therefore, to his own created temporal illusion. So music has, for the most part, ignored clock time and has used other means of rhythmic organization. Let us hear a musical illustration:

MOZART: *Symphony No. 40 in G Minor*, First Movement

As you listen to the music, what do you notice about the temporal aspect of the sound? This is a difficult question because it involves a very complex phenomenon. We shall soon see that rhythm is organized in several different layers, or levels of complexity. There are some features of the rhythmic organization, however, which are obvious. The most elementary level, and the easiest to grasp, is that the music seems to contain recurring beats or pulses. As you listen, it will be quite easy to tap your foot in time with the music. The greatest part of all the music ever written utilizes the beat. Listen to the third movement of the Mozart symphony; you will hear and feel the beat as in the first movement. Indeed, it would be difficult to find a piece of music in which the beat could not be found. We shall, for the moment, simply say that the beat is a basic phenomenon in the rhythmic organization of music. This beat is the unit of measurement for which we have been looking. It gives us a standard by which to measure the length of all the tones. With this constant unit of measurement, we may measure all tones in multiples or fractions of a beat.

Meter

*

To illustrate this second level of rhythmic organization, let us return to the first movement of the Mozart symphony. As you listen to the succession of beats you will notice that they do not seem to occur in isolation, but in groups. There is the distinct perception that the beats are occurring in groups of two in this music. What causes this to be true? We might say the first beat in each group is accented and the second is unaccented. A better description would be to speak of strong and weak beats. Something about the way the tones are perceived causes the first beat in each group to seem stronger.

To continue this point, listen again to the third movement of the symphony. As we hear the succession of beats we notice that they are again perceived in groups. This time, however, the beats seem to fall into groups of three, rather than two. In other words the beats are STRONG-weak-weak, rather than STRONG-weak. These are the only possibilities. The succession of beats within a piece will always occur in groups of two or of three. We shall presently see that these groups may occur in many different arrangements, yielding patterns of varying degrees of subtlety and complexity. But this one fact remains—beat groups are either duple or triple.

This phenomenon—the perception of beats in groups—is called meter. This is the second level of rhythmic organization. It is impossible to overstress the fact that both levels of rhythm we have discussed are subjective in nature. The beat may or may not actually be played. It may simply be inferred from the rhythmic flow of the music. The grouping of the beats, whether overt or implied, is never really done by the players. It is a matter of inference by the listener. It is an inference made possible by the tones being heard—an inference carefully encouraged by the manner in which the composer writes the music. The whole rhythmic and formal edifice of the composition must be constructed upon this intangible framework. But despite the subjective nature of these phenomena, they are basic to the composition of music and to its understanding.

To illustrate some of the possibilities inherent in these simple duple and triple groups, here is a more complex example:

TCHAIKOVSKY: *Symphony No. 6, Opus 74*, Second Movement

Listen carefully to the music until the beat is clearly heard and attempt to ascertain whether the beats fall into groups of two or of three. There is a rather obvious check for duple meter—simply imagine trying to march to the music. If this seems comfortable, with the strong beats always occurring on the motion of the same foot, the meter is duple. Since the only other choice is triple meter, an uncomfortable marching attempt could be expected to indicate triple meter. However, this test will work only if the metric groupings are consistent. But how does it seem to work in the case of this particular movement? Not very well. Try counting ONE-two, ONE-two to the music. This does not seem to work. Try counting ONE-two-three, ONE-two-three. This is no better. Now, if meter must be either duple or triple, and if neither test works, what is going on in this piece? The answer can be illustrated in the following way: Try counting ONE-two, ONE-two-three; ONE-two, ONE-two-three. The mystery is solved. The melody seems to occur with a metrical organization consisting of five beats in a series, with these being grouped 2+3. The rule that all beat groupings must be either duple or triple is preserved. But there is no rule that requires a piece of music to restrict itself entirely to one or the other. The metric groupings may be freely mixed and interchanged. In this case, the mixing of meters is accomplished in a completely regular manner. If you listen to the entire movement and analyze the metric structure, you will find the formula 2+3 to hold. This is a clear example of what may be called mixed regular meter.

The next example illustrates a more subtle metric situation:

CHAVEZ: *Sinfonia India*

You may find this to be a real metric challenge. Admittedly, the beats come by at a frantic rate of speed. But with a little patience and some extended experience listening to the music, they may be located.

After having become a bit more comfortable with the beats, we can begin to listen for the metric groupings. We apply the tests for duple and triple meter, and again our efforts seem to get us nowhere. This is apparently another case of mixed meter. The problem, then, is to find the formula by which the groups are mixed. In the previous example, we found this to be 2+3. Can we find a similar touchstone which will allow us to clarify the metric organization of this composition? We can analyze the metric organization and express it as a combination of duple and triple groups, but we are not able to find one formula which works for the entire composition.

The first several seconds may be diagrammed as 3+2+2+2+3+2+2+2+2+2+3+2+3+2+3+2+2+2+2. This indeed explains the rhythmic organization of those first few seconds, but does nothing to enlighten us about the rest of the composition. It provides no simple key to the total rhythmic organization. The reason is that this is an example of mixed irregular meter. Our inability to analyze this meter in a neat and simple manner is not a criticism of the music. The rhythmic organization is musically logical and is also interesting and exciting. It is the great variety of metric groupings—a variety which results in logical and comprehensible musical ideas—which accounts for the energy and excitement of the piece. This is a perfect example of music which achieves rhythmic interest by the alternation of meters.

Foreground Rhythm

*

Thus far we have observed two levels of rhythmic activity—the flow of beats and the meter. We have observed, also, that sometimes these two levels are not actually sounded, but are inferred by the listener from the actual tones played. What is played that encourages these inferences? The rhythm of the melody itself. Because of the nature of this phenomenon—the fact that this is the one level of rhythm that is actually being sounded—the term foreground rhythm seems descriptive and appropriate. This is the third level of rhythmic organization.

It can easily be seen that the three levels of rhythm—beat, meter, and foreground rhythm—can combine to make possible many varieties of rhythmic activity. It is also apparent that the types of interaction among these levels can be many and varied and that this interaction makes for rhythmic interest. To illustrate this, a simple experiment may be employed. For this purpose, three persons are needed. Choose a simple tune, such as *America*, *The Star Spangled Banner*, or *Yankee Doodle*. Let one person establish a flow of beats by tapping at a moderate speed. While this continues, the second person establishes the meter by stamping his foot lightly on the first beat of each metric group. Be careful at this point to make certain that the meter is correct—triple for *America* and *The Star Spangled Banner*, duple for *Yankee Doodle*. As the beat and meter continue, the third person claps the foreground rhythm that would be heard if the tune were sung. This can be diagrammed as follows:

AMERICA

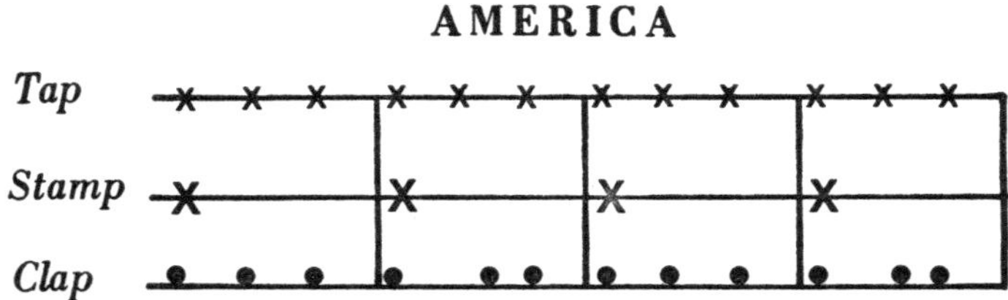

Ex. 4.1

Listen carefully to the way in which the three parts fit together. This is a very simple demonstration of the interaction between three levels of rhythmic organization.

The situation is not always this simple. The meter itself may be very complex, as it was in the *Sinfonia India*. The foreground rhythm may be complex in the extreme. And the interactions of these layers may be complicated and subtle. The possibilities for artistic use of these rhythmic principles are limited only by the imagination of the composer. But no matter how complex the rhythmic organization of a piece may become, it is still founded upon these three simple layers of rhythm and their interactions.

At this stage of our study, you should take time to go back to the examples used earlier in the chapter, play each one several times, and listen to the way the three levels of rhythm fit together. This will be fairly simple for Mozart, a little more difficult for Tchaikovsky, and quite complex for Chavez. You will learn much from the attempt and discover many interesting rhythmic phenomena of which you may not have been aware. This is the beginning of a habit of analytical listening which can open many previously closed doors of musical understanding.

ACHIEVING RHYTHMIC INTEREST

*

The composer has at his disposal many methods of achieving interest through the interactions among the three levels of rhythmic organization. Basic to all these is the element of surprise within the framework of a reasonably consistent pattern of metric groups. The secret is to have enough surprise to be interesting, but not so much that the hearer becomes disoriented and loses the ability to perceive the basic flow of beats and metric groups. Achievement of rhythmic interest depends primarily upon an understanding of ways in which strong beats can be delivered in places where weak beats are expected. Although there are many ways this may be done, they fall into three broad categories: mixed meters, beat displacement, and superimposition.

We have already seen examples of two kinds of mixed meters: the movement from the Tchaikovsky symphony and the *Sinfonia India* of Chavez. The Tchaikovsky movement employed meters in regular alternation, while the *Sinfonia India* employed no consistent pattern. If you will return for a moment to our discussion of that composition, you will recall that we analyzed the first few seconds as a very heterogeneous type of meter alternation. Our analysis revealed no regular pattern of alternation, but it did reveal another kind of rhythmic sense. Fourteen of the metric groups were duple, and triple groups occurred only occasionally. This is a way of employing the element of surprise and delivering strong beats in unexpected places.

Displacement

*

The category of beat displacement presents greater difficulties, partly because it is more subtle and complex and partly because there are so many different varieties. To illustrate the general idea, we turn to another experiment, again using the tune *America.* Three persons are needed, just as they were in our previous experiment. Again the first person taps the beat, the second stamps the meter, and the third claps the foreground rhythm. But this time, let the third person begin the foreground rhythm on the second beat of a group, rather than on the first. For the entire length of the tune the strong beats will fall upon beats which we expect to be weak. The strong beats have, in effect, been displaced, or moved over one beat from where they were expected. Of course a whole melody is rarely displaced. More often only a few beats, a single beat, or even a half-beat displacement will be found. Here is an example:

DEBUSSY: *Golliwog's Cake Walk*

The distinctive rhythmic flavor of this piece is attained through the use of a particular type of displacement known as syncopation. The displaced strong beats are moved out of position for only the space of a half-beat. This places the stress upon the second half of the beat, where no emphasis would be expected. This is difficult to explain in words, but the music speaks clearly for itself. Here is another example:

BRAHMS: *Intermezzo, Opus 76, No. 3*

Although the music sounds quite different from the previous

example, the same basic technique is employed. The player's left hand sounds a regular succession of duple beat groups. The right hand, however, begins on the second half of a group, thus placing strong beats where weak ones should be expected. This continues for four beat groups, and then the same rhythmic idea is begun again. Forty beat groups have gone by before this idea is temporarily abandoned.

This is difficult, but it is quite sufficient that you understand the basic idea and detect something of what is happening in the music. This skill will, of course, improve with more listening experience. To illustrate just how far this idea of beat displacement can go toward creating rhythmic variety and interest, let us listen to another example:

COPLAND: *El Salon Mexico*

Here is a brilliant display of rhythmic inventiveness. Displacements of every kind are combined with changing meters.

Superimposition

*

The third category of rhythmic device—superimposition—is made possible by the multi-voiced nature of music. Almost all music consists of several things going on at once, usually played by several instruments simultaneously. This makes possible a variety of rhythmic devices, including superimposition. Again we turn to an experiment, similar to the ones we have performed above. The first person again taps the flow of beats. This time the second performer stamps a duple meter. The third person claps a triple meter. If you listen carefully, you will hear the peculiar interaction of the two meters. Duple and triple groups, each based upon the same flow of beats, are superimposed upon each other. The resulting interplay of strong beats produces an interesting rhythmic effect. If you can imagine each of these meters becoming the basis for a foreground rhythm of its own, you can begin to sense the possibilities inherent in the idea of superimposition. To assist us in this, we hear another example:

BRAHMS: *Capriccio, Opus 76, No. 5*

The two meters are to be found distributed between the upper and lower voices. The left hand plays detached notes in a duple meter, while the right hand plays the main melodic line in a clear triple meter. From time to time the roles of the two hands are reversed, and occasionally the superimposition is abandoned entirely. But much of the piece contains this clear superimposition of duple and triple meters. This device is employed basically for the purpose of a certain kind of surprise. In the case of superimposition we have an interplay of strong beats accomplished in such a way that the strong beats in one meter fall upon the weak beats of the other. Here is a particularly sophisticated example of superimposed meters, which will serve to establish the point further:

BRAHMS: *Symphony No. 3, Opus 90*, Fourth Movement

This is a movement with as much rhythmic variety and interest as one could possibly desire. It begins in a straightforward manner in an easily detected duple meter. However, things change when the piece has continued for about one minute and twenty-five seconds. While the bass viols continue with the previously established duple meter, the other instruments play a new theme. The superimposition of the triple theme over the firmly established duple meter surprises the listener and adds musical interest.

Summary

*

At this point we have learned a great deal about musical rhythm. To summarize the main points, we have noted the three basic levels of beat, meter, and foreground rhythm. We have seen how the interaction of these three levels accounts for the rhythmic interest in music. Also, we have learned that an important principle in gaining rhythmic interest is delivering strong beats where weak ones are expected. Toward that end, we have seen several examples of the employment of mixed meters, beat displacements, and superimposition of meters. Rhythm is much more than a simple matter of measurement. In music, the time relationships between the duration of tones are of greater importance than having an absolute time value for each tone.

MELODY: THE MUSICAL LINE

MELODY

is the component of music most readily noticed and remembered. If you ask someone, "How does that piece go?" he will in all probability answer you by humming or whistling the melody. Of course there is always more to the composition than just the melody, but it is the most prominent and the most easily reproducible aspect of the piece. In most concert music melody's greatest importance lies in its thematic usage in building longer musical forms.

The melodies contained within a long composition constitute a sort of cast of characters about which the piece is written. Following the melodies of the composition throughout many appearances, disappearances, reappearances, and transformations is the central act of intelligent listening. So melody is a subject of great importance in understanding music.

Melody is one of the most difficult musical elements to discuss and explain. Why is a melody good or bad? What is there about some tunes that cause them to be moving and memorable? These questions are impossible to answer adequately. The ability to write good melodies seems to be a gift, possessed in varying degrees by different composers. This innate ability may be refined and improved through experience, but one either has it or one doesn't, and no amount of study and training can create it. This being the case, it is difficult, if not impossible, to identify the definitive criteria for a good melody. We can, however, analyze melody in a somewhat technical way in order to understand the basic principles involved, and we may listen to a few melodies which illustrate these principles.

MELODIC ELEMENTS

*

Reduced to its bare essentials, melody is **pitch** plus **rhythm.** We learned earlier that of the several layers of rhythmic activity within a piece, the one which we have called foreground rhythm was the only level always actually heard. This foreground rhythm plus a certain arrangement of pitches equals the melody. Melody is a certain rhythmic structure superimposed upon a certain pitch structure. An easy example comes to mind. Almost everyone knows the Christmas carol *Joy to the World.* The first phrase of that melody is a descending pattern of eight pitches, familiar to musicians as a descending major scale.

Ex. 5.1

If it is sung or played without rhythm, it is readily recognizable, but only as a descending major scale, not as *Joy to the World.* Only when the rhythm is superimposed upon it does it reveal itself as a recognizable melody.

Ex. 5.2

So melody, in its simplest aspect, consists of two basic features: **pitch and rhythm**. The composer's manipulation of either of these elements makes a profound impact upon the ultimate character of the melody.

Melodic Contour

*

These basic elements of pitch and rhythm are combined to produce many other features of melodic structure. One of these is **contour**–the shape of the melody. This may seem strange since we are not accustomed to speaking of the shape of something which is heard rather than seen. It must be admitted that the term is most often used to refer to the melody as it appears in notation, a visual rather than an aural phenomenon. But the notion of shape applies, although in a somewhat more metaphoric sense, to the sound of the melody itself. This is most readily demonstrable in the matter of melodic **direction.** A melody may move in only three directions. It may move upward; it may move downward; or it may remain at the same pitch level by repeating tones. Of course any melody worthy of the name must use all three. A tune can go in one direction for only a very limited time before some directional change is necessary. This is true not only because a melody moving in the same direction would soon exhaust the range of the instrument playing it, but because such a melody would soon become intolerably dull.

The achievment of a melodic line pleasing to the ear requires a mixture of ascending, descending, and repeated tone motion. Nevertheless, many melodies are constructed so that one of these types of motion is more prominent than the others, and such construction is usually important to the effect of the melody. *Joy to the World* not only begins with a descending melody; descending melodic construction predominates throughout the entire song, even though many repeated tones and ascending patterns are used. In the same fashion, the last movement of Mozart's *Symphony No. 40 in g minor* begins with a melody which is ascending, and ascending motion characterizes the entire theme.

Ex. 5.3

In addition to direction, contour also involves at least two other dimensions: **range** and **type of movement**. The **range** of a melody refers to the distance between the highest and lowest notes contained within it. This can be seen visually in two ways. It can be observed as notation, or it can be seen more graphically by watching the melody being played on the piano. The wider the range of the melody, the more "territory" is covered on the piano keyboard. But it can also be heard, as well as seen. This may take some practice and some unusual concentration, but it is possible. The two examples we have just cited, *Joy to the World* and the Mozart symphony both cover a fairly wide range; they are wide melodies. In contrast, *America* and *Yankee Doodle* are narrow melodies; they cover a narrower range and seem to hover around just a few pitches. Example 5.4 shows, in graph form, the differences in the melodic ranges of the first phrase of each of the songs.

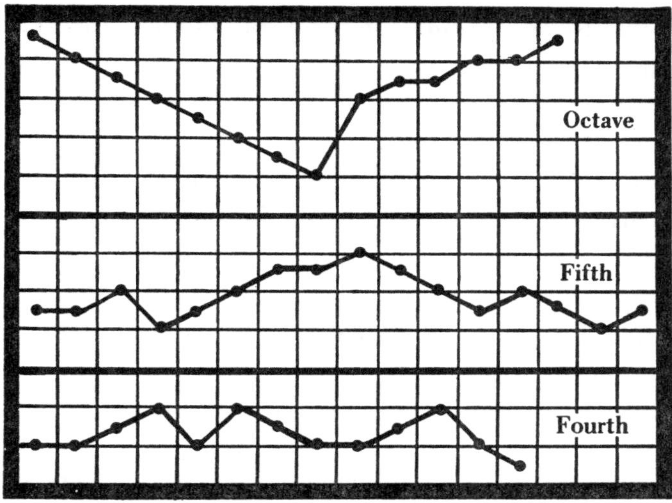

Ex. 5.4

The concept which we have called **type of movement** is more difficult to comprehend. To understand it, we must first touch upon the subject of musical scales. We noted previously that the pitch of a tone depends upon the frequency of the vibrations associated with it. Theoretically, an infinite number of pitches is available. Just as there is no theoretical limit to the frequencies which may be produced by vibrating bodies, there is no limit to the corresponding pitches. Even if we restrict ourselves to those frequencies audible to the human ear, roughly 20-20,000 vibrations per second, there is still theoretically possible an infinite number of pitches between these limits, since we may divide this range fractionally in a limitless number of ways.

If there is an infinite universe of pitches theoretically available, the composer must find some way of organizing this material. For this reason many systems have evolved for limiting the material to a much smaller number of pitches and for arranging these pitches into an organized tonal system. The particular system, which we in the so-called Western World have inherited, consists of twelve pitches. This can be illustrated visually by looking at the piano keyboard in Example 5.5. You will notice that the keys are arranged in such a way that the series of white notes is interspaced with black notes in alternating groups of two and three. You will also notice that this arrangement repeats itself every twelve keys. This represents the twelve pitches available in our system—the pitches making up the so-called chromatic scale.

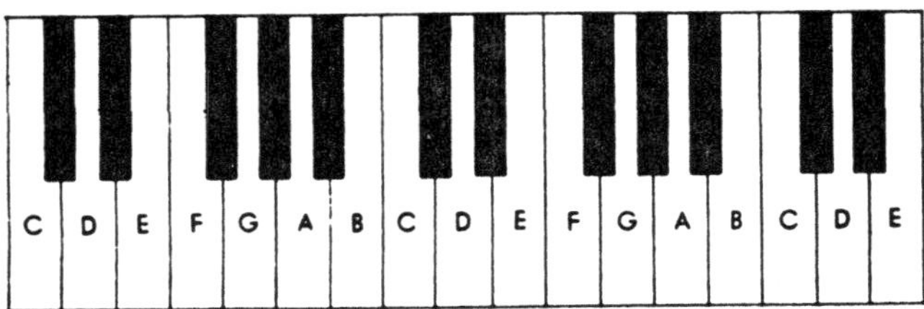

Ex. 5.5

In actual practice the composer usually further limits his choice of pitches to a smaller number chosen from these twelve and arranged into a systematic grouping known as a scale. Many different arrangements are possible, and many different scales have been formed from the available twelve tones. The most common scales in ordinary use consist of eight tones, arranged in certain patterns. To understand this, we must first understand the concept of whole and half steps. Referring again to Example 5.5, we can use the piano keyboard as a tool. The distance from any key on the keyboard to any adjacent key is called the interval of a half step. In most cases, this will be from a white key to a black key or from a black key to a white one. There are places on the keyboard, however, where two white keys are adjacent, with no black key intervening. In these cases the distance between the two white keys is a half step. The principle is invariable: a half step is the distance between any two adjacent keys. A whole step is simply two half steps.

The character of a scale depends upon the distribution of half steps and whole steps. The most common scale, known as the major scale, is distributed as follows:

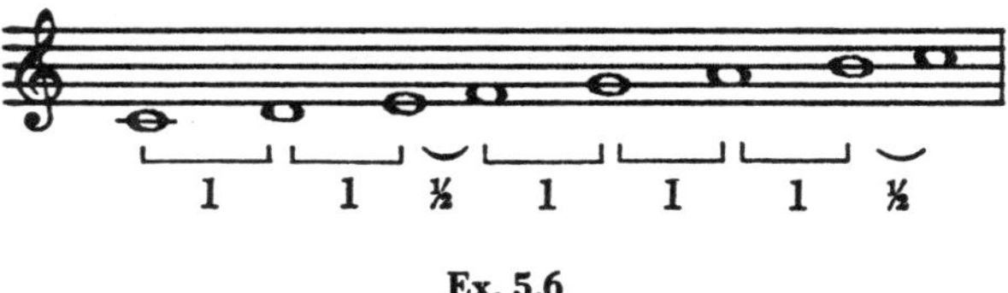

Ex. 5.6

Another common scale is the natural minor scale:

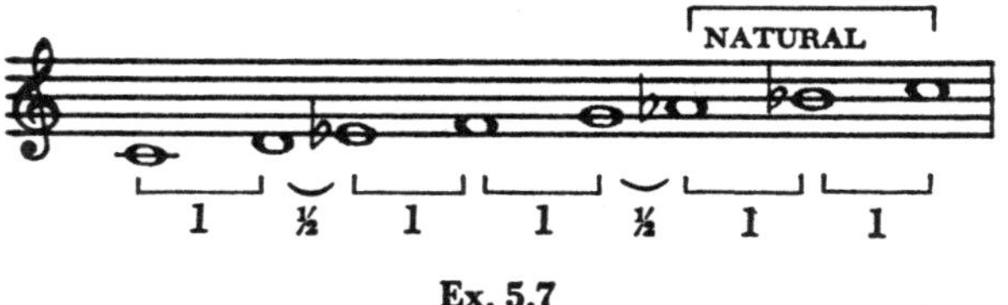

Ex. 5.7

A variation of this scale is the harmonic minor, in which the seventh degree of the scale is raised a half step:

Ex. 5.8

The character of a scale is directly dependent upon this distribution of intervals, or distances between the various tones. When we speak of intervals, it is helpful to be able to label them. This we do by simply counting up the number of lines and spaces between the two tones in question. For example, the two tones below define an interval covering a total of three spaces and lines:

Ex. 5.9

Therefore, this interval is called a *third.* The following interval covers five lines and spaces:

Ex. 5.10

It is the interval of a fifth. The same principle applies in labelling all intervals.

Having become acquainted with this basic concept of scale and interval, we can now understand the characteristic of melody which we have called type of movement. Movement may be of two types: stepwise and skipwise. Stepwise melody follows the outline of the scale; each tone progresses to the tone next to it in the scale. It moves by intervals of a second. Skipwise melody moves in intervals of a third or wider. It progresses from one tone to another tone farther away than the next adjacent tone. It skips some of the degrees of the scale. In actual practice, just as a melody never moves only in one direction, it almost never moves entirely by either stepwise or skipwise motion. Still, most melodies feature one type of motion more than the other, and the type of motion which predominates influences the contour of the melody, and the effect which the melody produces.

The contour of the melody, then, consists of three main features: the **direction**, which may be ascending, descending, or by repeated tones; the **range** or width; and the **motion**, which may be either by step or by skip. Perhaps more than any other feature of the melody, contour determines its effect and quality.

Melodic Length

*

Another important feature of melody which should be noted is **length**. Again, as with contour, this is a concept of space which applies equally well to sound. How can we measure the length of a melody? How can we tell when a melody is finished? To understand this, we can perform a simple experiment. Sing *America.* As you approach the line "of Thee I sing" stop one word short. Sing, "of Thee I . . . " You will feel uncomfortable, not only because the sentence is incomplete, but because the music itself seems to want to move on farther. If you then complete the line, you will find that a sense of rest or completion seems to occur. This resting point in the melody is called a cadence. Each degree of the scale has certain tendencies which result in motion toward the first degree, or tonic. The cadence is reached on the word "sing" because the tonic note is sounded on that word, having been immediately preceded on "I" by the seventh degree, the tone of the scale which produces the greatest degree of motion toward the tonic. This is called the principle of tonality. A melody which moves for a long period of time before reaching a cadence is a long melody; one which reaches a cadence rather quickly is a short melody. Length of melody is not ordinarily measured by clock time, but by the number of beat groups which it contains. The phrase of *America* just sung occupies six beat groups.

Melodic Character

*

The third major feature of melody is one which is difficult to define and name. For want of a better term, let us call it character. By character we mean the total of qualities, objective and subjective, which are associated with the melody. This includes contour and length, as well as many other aspects of the melody, both tonal and rhythmic. It includes the sum of all descriptive statements that may be made about a given melody.

These three major melodic features—contour, length, and character may be better understood through the use of some comparative examples. Let us analyze three pieces which display different melodic contours:

WEBERN: *Symphony No. 1 for Small Orchestra, Opus 21*

BACH: *Brandenberg Concerto No. 6*, Second Movement

MOZART: *Symphony No. 40 in G Minor*, Fourth Movement

These three compositions display obvious differences in contour. The Bach concerto moves predominantly by step, while both the Mozart and Webern examples move by skip. The Mozart example moves smoothly upward over a wide range. The Webern melody is not smooth, but angular. Of course, this description is metaphoric, but it does represent the sounds being heard. Now to illustrate from actual musical literature the notion of length, we turn to some further examples:

BEETHOVEN: *Symphony No. 8, Opus 93*, First Movement

BACH: *Brandenburg Concerto No. 3*, First Movement

WAGNER: *Die Meistersinger*, Prelude to Act III

Length of a melody can be determined only if the cadences can be clearly heard. There is great difference in the clarity of cadences between these three compositions. The cadences in the Beethoven symphony are clear and easy to hear. The cadences in the Bach concerto are clear, but more difficult to find, since a technique of delaying the cadences is employed. Those in the Wagner are more obscure and difficult to locate.

The melody in the Beethoven symphony is short, or to be more accurate, consists of very short segments marked by clear cadences. The melody of the Bach concerto is longer, and it is made longer by a very clever device. The melody gains length by a technique of delayed cadence. The composer leads us to believe a cadence is about to occur, and then continues the melody before actually reaching the cadence. It is as if you were about to sit in a chair, when suddenly someone picked you up by the collar and sets you scuffling along to the next chair. The effect is one of lengthening the melody and of heightening interest by an element of surprise, a principle which we found to be important during our discussion of rhythm. The Wagner example consists of very long melodic segments. This is accomplished in a different way from the technique used in the Brandenburg concerto. Wagner's is attained by avoiding the cadence altogether for long periods of time. Rather than being surprised only once, we are constantly expecting to hear a cadence that seems never to come. This example very nearly attains the "endless melody" of which Wagner was so fond. Now we attack the concept of melodic character:

BEETHOVEN: *Symphony No. 3, Opus 55*, Second Movement

BEETHOVEN: *Symphony No. 3, Opus 55*, Third Movement

DEBUSSY: *Pagodes*

DEBUSSY: *Cloches à travers les feuilles*

It is obvious that these melodies sound very different from each other. We could cite differences in contour and length, and these do influence the character, or effect of the melody.

There are other factors, however, which bear upon the melodic character. If you were called upon to describe the character of these pieces by assigning adjectives to them, you could well call the first one sad, the second one gay, the third oriental, and the last one wistful or dream-like. What contributes to these differences? Without doubt the rhythm is important. The slowness of the first example helps give it the character of a funeral march, which indeed it is. The fast tempo of the third movement of the Beethoven symphony, combined with the light manner of playing, tends to give a puckish and joking effect. The relatively static character of the movement within both the Debussy examples contributes to their placid quality.

There is another important element entering into these examples which helps determine the character of the melodies—scale. We saw earlier that a composer usually limits his tonal material to a number of tones fewer than the twelve available to him. As a rule he chooses a scale of seven tones. Sometimes he may use even fewer. The choice of scale greatly influences the character of the melody. The Beethoven funeral march uses a minor scale, which is an important factor in the somber and funereal tone of the melody. The third movement of the Beethoven symphony uses the major scale—a brighter sound. The Debussy *Pagodes* uses a pentatonic, or five-tone, scale usually thought of as oriental in nature. *Cloches à travers les feuilles* employs a six-tone scale, called the whole-tone scale. Its peculiar character stems from the complete absence of half steps. This means that all the tones of the scale are an equal distance (a whole step) apart. The result is a static feeling, with little tonal tendency of motion toward a tonic center.

As you can see, the thing which we call melodic character is complex, and even subjective. It includes everything that can be said or described about a melody. It is an attempt to describe a melody in every possible way.

These features—contour, length, character—are aspects of melody which are subject to description and analysis. They help us to discuss melody and to describe melodic styles.

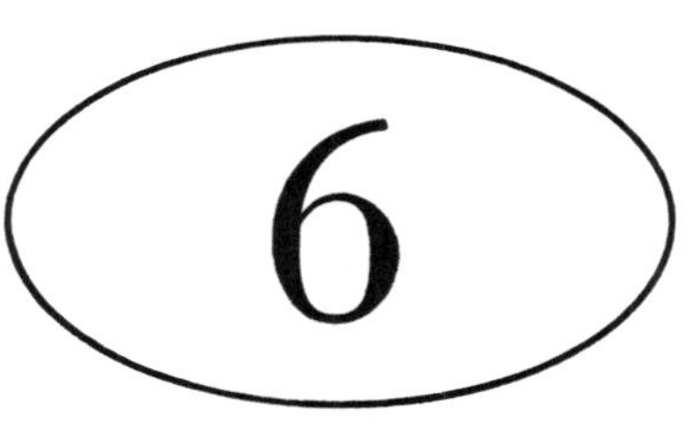

TEXTURE: THE COMBINATION OF LINES

As we continue our study of the elements of music, we are discovering the manner in which music is put together. We first became acquainted with the most basic aspect of music—rhythm. Next we learned how the tonal element, or pitch, could be combined with rhythm to produce melody. This has brought us to an understanding of any music which consists of a single melodic line-music which can be whistled, hummed, sung, or played by a single instrument such as a trumpet or clarinet. But most music is more complex than this; it involves many instruments playing at the same time, and playing more than one melodic line simultaneously.

MUSICAL TEXTURE

*

The next step in our broadening understanding must be the study of **musical texture**: the ways in which melodic lines may be combined. To grasp the concept of musical texture, we must first understand the idea of melodic line. Let us suppose we are listening to a song being sung by one person.

Obviously, we can be hearing only one melody, or one line. If a second person joins in and harmonizes with the first, we are hearing two lines. A third person joining the harmony would produce a third line. This assumes that each of the singers is singing a different part and not just singing the same melody in unison. If many persons are all singing the same melody, we are still hearing only one melodic line. The same thing is true of an instrumental ensemble, such as the orchestra. For example, there are many violas, and they usually play the same notes at the same time. This produces only one melodic line, regardless of the number of instruments involved.

Most music consists of several lines sounding at once. Let us listen to several compositions illustrating different textures:

VARESE: *Density 21.5*

BEETHOVEN: *Quartet No. 14, Opus 131*, First Movement

WAGNER: *Lohengrin*, Prelude to Act III

STRAUSS: *Also sprach Zarathustra, Opus 30*

Density

*

These examples illustrate several features of musical texture. First, we can discriminate between different degrees of **density**—the thickness or thinness of sound. The thinnest texture is *Density 21.5*, which consists of a single line played by a single instrument. The texture of the Beethoven quartet is thicker, consisting of four lines played by four instruments. *Also sprach Zarathustra* is the thickest texture, because it consists of the greatest number of lines.

Range

*

There is another feature of texture which influences the sound profoundly, but which is not a matter of thickness or thinness. This is **range**—the tonal distance from the lowest voice to the highest. The *Lohengrin* prelude begins with all the lines being played in a high pitch range. The effect is conveyed not only by the high pitch, but also by the limited range of the texture. The tonal distance from the lowest voice to the highest is narrow. *Also sprach Zarathustra*, on the other hand, covers the widest imaginable range, from the growling contrabassoon to the first violins and trumpets. These examples illustrate density and range in a very clear way. We should not leave the impression that the situation is always so simple. Density and range may interact in a variety of ways. Suppose a piece uses, at any given time, only a very low and a very high line with nothing between. This would give a wide range, but would still result in a thin sound. On the other hand, a texture might be quite thick and still cover a relatively narrow range if many voices are written very close together in pitch.

Textural Type

*

In addition to density and range, there are other important textural considerations. The most important of these is **textural type**. To illustrate this aspect of texture an analogy may be drawn. A piece of cloth may be either wide or narrow; a piece of music may employ a wide or a narrow range. The cloth may be of coarse weave or of fine; the music may be of thick texture or of thin. Independent of these factors, the cloth may have a certain pattern woven into it. Similarly, a piece of music may employ a particular type of texture. Three such basic types of musical texture may be identified. This may be illustrated by the following examples:

VARESE: *Density 21.5*

WAGNER: *Parsifal*, Prelude to Act I, Opening Section

Both of these examples consist of a single line of music. *Density 21.5* is played by a single instrument. The opening seconds of *Parsifal* are played by an entire orchestral section, but still are only one line, since all the instruments are playing the same melody. These are illustrations of the simplest of the three basic types of texture—**monophonic texture.** Monophonic texture consists of a single line.

HANDEL: *Messiah*, He Shall Feed His Flock

HANDEL: *Messiah*, Pastoral Symphony

BEETHOVEN: *Symphony No. 8, Opus 93*, First Movement

The texture of these examples is more complex than the monophonic pieces we have just heard. Obviously, more than one line is involved here. But even in these more complex pieces, one line predominates over the others. In each case the texture consists of one predominant line with the others serving as accompaniment. This is illustrative of **homophonic texture**—one melody dominating the texture, with the other lines subordinated to it.

HANDEL: *Messiah*, And the Glory of the Lord

BACH: *Brandenberg Concerto No. 2*, Third Movement

This third type of musical texture is the most complex. Rather than having only one line, or one predominant line with subordinate accompaniment, there are many lines of equal importance. To illustrate this, put yourself in the position of a player or singer. In homophonic music the players performing the main melodic line would have far more interesting parts to play than would the players assigned the accompanying parts. In music of the type represented by these examples, all the players would be equally employed, because each of the lines is of equal importance. This is called **polyphonic texture**—a texture consisting of many equal lines.

In actual practice, music may not illustrate any of these three textural types in a pure form. It is more likely to use all these in various combinations during the course of a composition. Much music is constructed in such a subtle way that it is difficult to identify which basic texture is being used at a given time. The possible variations of texture are unlimited.

Polyphonic Devices

We have now identified three main considerations in our study of musical texture: density, range, and textural type. The composer may use a variety of devices as he weaves his musical fabric within the context of these main textural features. We shall examine many of these devices in detail when we discuss thematic processes later in the book, but some of them bear so importantly upon the subject of texture that we should discuss them briefly here. These techniques are often referred to as **polyphonic devices** because of their origins in polyphonic music and their extensive usage in polyphonic composition. However, most may also be used within the context of other textures.

The first device which we shall discuss is **imitation**. This is a true polyphonic device, because its use produces a polyphonic texture in every instance. An example will illustrate clearly what we mean by imitation:

HANDEL: *Messiah*, And With His Stripes

As each voice part enters, it sings the same line, or at least an identifiable part of the same line, which has been sung by the previous voice. Each voice imitates the previous one, hence the name imitation. This produces a polyphonic texture, because it gives equal importance to all the lines. This is the same technique that is used in the familar rounds such as *Row, Row, Row Your Boat.* It is a technique indispensable to the composer who wishes to write extended and complex works.

The other polyphonic devices are somewhat more complex. They can best be understood if we divide them into two classes—those which change the pitch structure and those which alter the rhythm.

The devices which deal with the pitch structure are **inversion** and **retrograde**. Inversion is simply what the name says—the playing of a melody upside down. If a melody is played so that every time it should move up it moves down instead, and vice versa, the melody is being played in inversion. Retrograde is the playing of a melody backwards. If the melody is played using the same rhythm but playing the pitches beginning at the end and working toward the beginning, the melody is being played in retrograde. In notation, these devices would appear as follows:

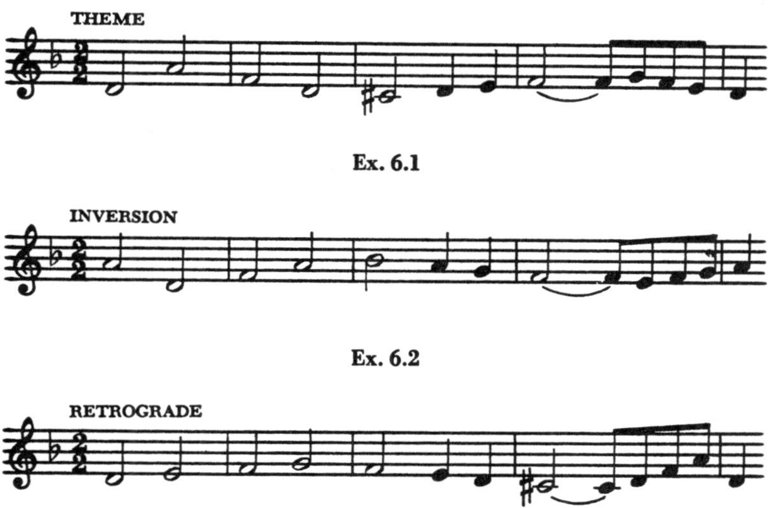

Ex. 6.1

Ex. 6.2

Ex. 6.3

The polyphonic devices which concern rhythm are **augmentation** and **diminution**. Augmentation is the playing of a melody in note values longer than those in the original. Diminution is just the reverse: the playing of a melody in note values shorter than those in the original theme. These devices are comparative and depend for their effectiveness upon the clear establishment of the basic tempo of the melodies to be augmented or diminished. Here are examples in notation, applying these devices to the same theme:

Ex. 6.4

Ex. 6.5

For actual musical examples which illustrate these devices, we turn to a composition by Johann Sebastian Bach.

BACH: *The Art of Fugue*, Contrapunctus One

BACH: *The Art of Fugue*, Contrapunctus Three

Contrapunctus One sets out the theme and develops it in a polyphonic texture. Contrapunctus Three uses the same theme in inversion.

BACH: *The Art of Fugue*, Contrapunctus Seven

This illustrates the use of augmentation. After the basic thematic material has been introduced, the theme appears in augmented form, beginning in the lowest voice and then passing through each of the voices in ascending order.

BACH: *The Art of Fugue*, Contrapunctus Six

This illustration of diminution requires some diligent listening. The theme (heard in Contrapunctus One) is embellished by the other voices playing the theme in diminution.

These devices illustrate the range of textural possibilities open to the skillful composer. Not only can they be used in their pure form, but some of the devices are compatible with others. Inversion may be combined with either augmentation or diminution, for example. Their importance lies not in the technical fact of their mere existence, but in the artistic uses to which the composer puts them. This is a subject to be explored in more depth when we discuss thematic processes in greater detail.

We have been introduced to the basic aspects of texture and some textural devices and noted that in actual practice it is rare to find any of these aspects of texture in their pure form. Rather, we usually find complex combinations and permutations of these basic features. In order to clarify this let us turn to another example and attempt to describe the features of its texture.

BACH: *Suite No. 3 in D*, Air

Although we may classify this texture as basically polyphonic, on first hearing this may not be readily apparent.

You may be tempted to say that it is homophonic, that it is one melody with subordinate accompaniment. But the melody is not as simple as it first sounds. Careful listening will reveal that it is accompanied by a second melody, or counter-melody, in the next highest line—the second violins. It is the combination of this melody and counter melody that gives the composition its lyric quality. Without either of these the piece would sound empty and less interesting. These lines are truly of equal importance, so we may classify the basic texture as polyphonic.

But there are other important textural features. The consistent "walking bass" appearing in the lowest voice of the orchestra is a vital part of the texture. So is the "fill-in" provided by the remaining lines of the orchestra. So we can see that this composition, even though justifiably classified as polyphonic contains some features of homophonic texture as well. The result is a texture more complex than any of the simple types we have discussed. This is a clear example of musical texture as it is usually found. It shows how basic textural types and devices may be mixed to produce a unique musical fabric, one which is characteristic of a single piece of music. The basic concepts of musical texture are common to all composition. The skillful fabrication of an interesting musical texture is one of the main goals of every composer.

HARMONY: THE VERTICAL ASPECT OF TEXTURE

To begin our study of harmony, we must return momentarily to the subject of line. We learned in the previous chapter that music consists of melodic lines, and that most music is made up of several lines sounding at once. This aspect of music is often referred to as being horizontal. This can be seen graphically by referring to Example 7.1. This is the score, or printed music page, for a composition by Handel. This is only a small part of the music, which would last only a few seconds. It would take sixty such pages to complete this particular concerto.

CONCERTO, No. 1

Ex. 7.1

The score consists of seven printed lines, corresponding to the seven melodic lines which are heard. You can follow each of these from left to right, and each represents a single line of music. This horizontal movement of the eye in following the lines is a clear illustration of the reason for referring to the movement of the line as horizontal. However, there is also a vertical aspect to the music. At any given instant in time, many lines are sounding simultaneously. This too can be seen on the printed score. If you scan the page in a vertical direction, you can see which note is being played in each of the lines at any given time. This requires a vertical eye movement, representing the vertical nature of texture.

THE TONAL SYSTEM

A little thought will reveal the importance of the vertical aspect of musical texture. Some lines combine well, while others do not. If you begin singing *Row, Row, Row Your Boat* and another person begins the same tune at the proper point, the two lines will fit together well. You will be performing a simple polyphonic form we call a round. If, on the other hand, the second person chooses to sing *America*, the two lines will clash badly. This admittedly ludicrous example should make the point. There is an art involved in fitting together two or more musical lines. This art is known as counterpoint. The particular part of this art dealing with vertical relationships is called harmony. Many harmonic systems have been devised. As an example, we shall briefly explore the one which has produced the largest body of Western music, including practically all popular music.

Chord Structure

*

The basic unit of any harmonic system is the chord. A chord is simply the sounding together of several tones. Suppose we begin with one tone:

Ex. 7.2 

We can construct a chord upon this "root" tone by adding two other tones, one the interval of a third above the root and the other a third above this first added tone (a fifth above the root). This will appear as follows:

Ex. 7.3 

Such a simple, three-tone chord is called a triad. We may add other tones to create more complex chords. If we add a tone the interval of a seventh above the root, the resulting chord is called a seventh chord:

Ex. 7.4 

If we add a ninth above the root, we have a ninth chord:

Ex. 7.5 

The same principle extends to building eleventh chords, thirteenth chords, and so on as far as we wish to go.

It is interesting to note that we can, applying this principle, build a chord on each degree of a scale; that is to say that we can use each degree of the scale as a root for a chord. Suppose we begin with a C Major scale:

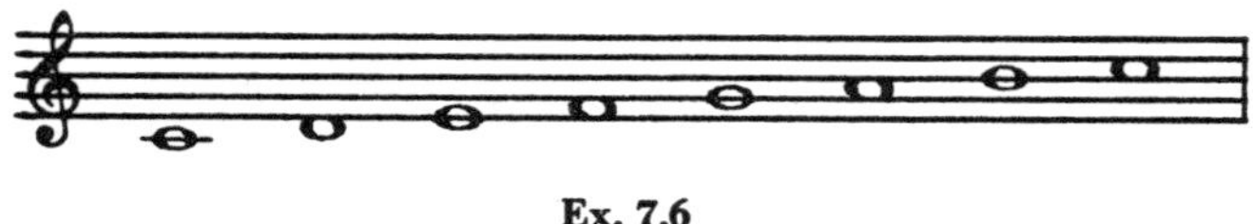

Ex. 7.6

We can build a chord on each degree:

Ex. 7.7

This gives us a rather complete harmonic system for the key of C Major. We can, of course, extend this idea and build seventh chords, ninth chords, or any other type of chord on each degree of the scale. If a composer writes in the key of C Major, he will, for the most part at least, use these chords; they are the chords which establish the key of C Major.

An additional quality of all chords is that they retain their identity and function even if the chord tones are arranged in different order. The root of the chord need not always be the bottom tone. This is called **inversion** and allows tones of one chord to lead more smoothly to tones of the next chord. The tones of the C and F chords may be written in the following manner:

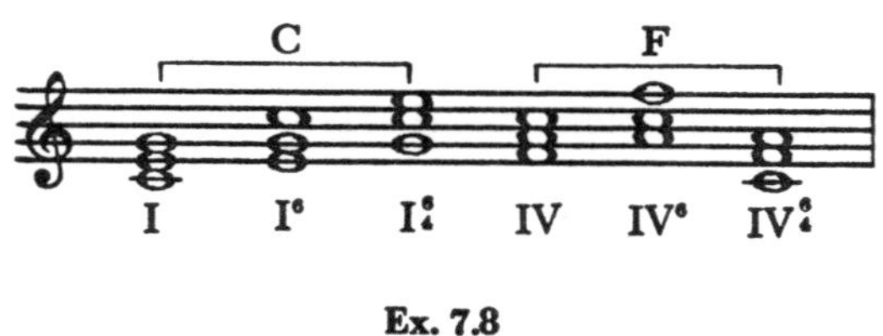

Ex. 7.8

But no matter what the arrangement of the tones, they still function as the I and IV chords in the key of C.

Harmonic Progression

*

The structure of this harmonic system results in an important phenomenon. You recall that in our previous discussion of tonality we discovered that each of the scale degrees had certain properties. The first degree served as a tonic, with the others tending to move toward that tonal center. The same thing is true in the case of chords within a given key. The chord constructed upon the first degree of the scale serves as a strong tonal center. Only when this chord is reached is there a feeling of complete rest and resolution. The other chords within the system tend to move toward the tonic.

Harmonic theorists have classified the chords of the tonal system according to their tendency to produce motion. The chords built on the fifth and seventh scale degrees, because they contain the leading tone, exhibit the strongest tendency to move directly to the tonic. Those built on the second and fourth scale degrees move normally toward those built on the fifth and seventh scale degrees. The entire codification of the system is quite complex, but this is sufficient to illustrate the essential point; the different chords of the harmonic system have different properties, and the result is the phenomenon known as **harmonic progression.** Harmonic progression is important in producing motion in music. It is a great reinforcement of the principle of tonality.

A composer is free, of course, to employ any of the chords within a tonal system in whatever way his creative urge suggests. In addition, he is not limited to these chords contained within a particular key, but may borrow chords from keys other than the one in which he is writing at the moment, and may make many other variations and alterations of the basic chords. This is beyond the scope of this book, however, and for further information you should refer to one of the books on harmony listed in the bibliography.

Modulation

*

We should, however, discuss one important harmonic technique before leaving the subject: the technique known as **modulation.** Modulation simply means the changing of key center within a piece of music. When a composer modulates, he is simply substituting the tones and chords of one key for those of another. For example, suppose the piece has been in the key of C Major, using this scale:

Ex. 7.9

The basic triads available are:

Ex. 7.10

Now, suppose the composer wished to change to the key of F Major, which is based upon this scale:

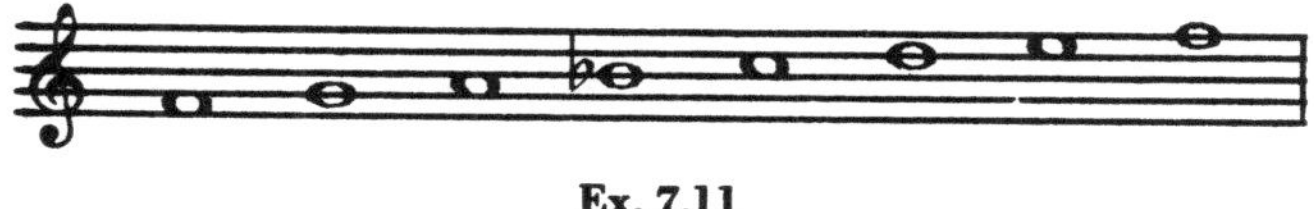

Ex. 7.11

The F Major scale contains these basic triads:

Ex. 7.12

There are several ways in which this could be done, but two are most common. The first is called **common chord modulation**. This is a way of changing keys by using a chord contained in both keys as a pivot point. For example, you will notice that the keys of C Major and F Major share several chords in common:

Ex. 7.13

Any of these could serve as the pivot for a common chord modulation. Here is an example of one such progression:

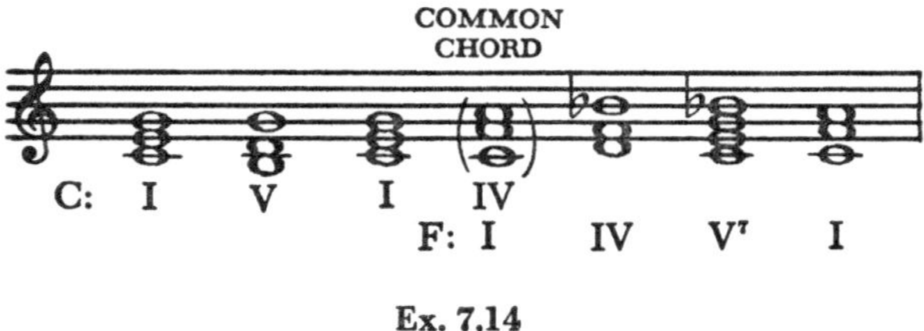

Ex. 7.14

A second type of modulation is called **chromatic modulation**. This uses a scale tone not contained within the original key. For example we might cite the following example of a chromatic modulation from C Major to the distantly related key of E Major:

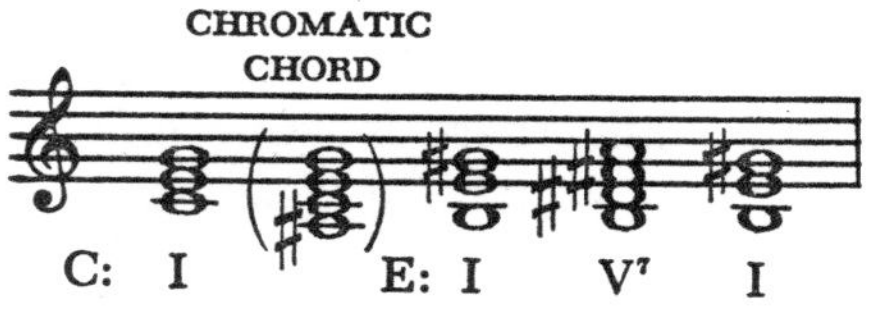

Ex. 7.15

The A sharp is contained in neither the key of C Major or E Major, and within the space of only five chords, the tonal center is changed from a key with no sharps or flats to a key with four sharps. The two keys share no common chords.

The possibilities inherent within the tonal system are limitless, but this should serve to give some hint of its nature. It should be borne in mind that the system outlined here is only one of many. Some twentieth century composers have employed chords built in fourths, rather than thirds. Some non-Western music employs no harmony at all. We discuss this particular harmonic system only because of its use in the largest body of music ordinarily heard in everyday life.

We have seen how harmonic progression adds to the movement of music. Harmony has another important function. It serves to add color. These two functions of harmony exist in varying proportions in every piece which employs harmony at all. For an example:

MOZART: *Symphony No. 40 in G Minor*, First Movement

The harmonic usage in this piece is predominantly one of providing motion. While there is some color added by the harmony, this of minor importance. Here are two other examples:

DEBUSSY: *La Cathédrale engloutie*

DEBUSSY: *Reflets dans l'eau*

In these two pieces, color is of paramount importance. The motion-giving properties of the harmonic progressions are of secondary importance.

FUNDAMENTALS OF MUSICAL FORM

MUSICAL STRUCTURE AND STYLE

We have been studying, up to this point, the fundamentals of music. This has included a study of the basic material of music—sound; consideration of the elements of music—rhythm, melody, and harmony; and an introduction to musical texture. This knowledge is prerequisite to an understanding of form and style. Form is a most important feature of any serious work of art. It is the carrier of the meaning and value of the work. The elements of an art do not take on meaning until the artist imposes form and order upon them. Art is the antithesis of chaos. The alternative to chaos is form.

Form exists upon several levels, upon the basic level of materials and upon the higher level of artistic elements. To illustrate this we turn for the moment to a consideration of form in several arts. Perhaps the easiest example to understand is to be found in architecture. As a building is constructed, it takes shape by brick laid upon brick and board being laid upon board. Large numbers of bricks combine to form a wall; walls combine to form wings; and wings combine to form a building. This is form on the level of materials. The thing which gives a building its character, however, is of higher order. It depends not only upon these basic materials, but more importantly upon the ways in which the materials are used. What differentiates Notre Dame from the Astrodome? The materials do play a part, to be sure. But more important than this, the buildings are differentiated by the basic forms. The planners of the two buildings had different ideas and goals. The materials were deployed in such manner as to realize these ideas. The important differentiator is the idea, not just the materials. So form exists as a juxtaposition of ideas and elements. It is not only the relation of stone to stone that makes Notre Dame; it is the relation of architectural elements: the spires, the buttresses, the windows, and the general shaping of space as well as the architectural materials that makes Notre Dame what it is.

Similarly, the materials of painting are paint and canvas. But it can hardly be said that the form of a great painting is merely the distribution of the former upon the latter. The important formal features of a painting are the ways in which the elements—line, color, space, shape—are deployed. A painting is great not because of the paint; it is great because the elements are combined to make a coherent and meaningful form. It is not just that the painting depicts a certain scene or a certain person. The same thing could be done in the most informal and unplanned snapshot. It is the conscious selection of pictorial elements and the imposing of form upon them that produces meaning and value. Now let us consider form in poetry. Here is a famous poem by Shelley:

OZYMANDIAS

I met a traveler from an antique land A
Who said: Two vast and trunkless legs of stone B
Stand in the desert. Near them, on the sand, A
Half sunk, a shattered visage lies, whose frown, B
And wrinkled lip, and sneer of cold command, A
Tell that its sculptor well those passions read C
Which yet survive, stamped on these lifeless things, D
The hand that mocked them and the heart that fed; C
And on the pedestal these words appear: E
"My name is Ozymandias, king of kings: D
Look on my works, ye Mighty, and despair!" E
Nothing beside remains. Round the decay F
Of that colossal wreck, boundless and bare E
The lone and level sands stretch far away. F

The basic material of poetry is words. And, accordingly, the words of this poem and their deployment are important, particularly the constant ten-syllable line and the subtle rhyme scheme. But the work certainly consists of more than just this. It is the use and handling of all the poetic elements that produces the impact of the poem. The vivid imagery creates a feeling for the power of the king, Ozymandias. This is followed by a reminder that his might is already gone and forgotten. The picture of this might is built up through the use of long and complex sentences, followed by the incisive and stark "Nothing beside remains." This, in turn, followed by a brief denouement produces the overpowering feeling of emptiness and futility which characterizes the poem. Of course words, basic material, carry this meaning. But it is much more than words. Shelley could have said, "All fame and power are temporary." But the effect would not have been the same. It was the shaping of all the poetic elements that produced the meaning. It was form.

ELEMENTS OF FORM

*

The same is true of music. The basic material of music is sound. But musical form is more than just the deployment of sound in time. It is the use and the arrangement of musical elements—melodies, rhythms, harmonies. It is the handling of basic musical ideas, or themes. It is the building up, idea upon idea, of a complex structure whose meaning lies in the relationship of one element to another and the relationship of each element to the whole. This is done in the same general way as in the other arts. Just as architecture lays brick upon brick to produce a wall, and wall beside wall to produce a building, music lays its building blocks upon each other to produce larger and larger units.

The Phrase

The basic unit of music is the **phrase**. A phrase is the smallest unit which produces a complete musical thought. The end of a phrase is marked by a cadence at which point the melody, harmony, and rhythm come to a partial or complete rest. Phrases combine to make phrase groups; phrase groups combine to make sections; these combine to make larger sections; and so on until the complete musical composition is built. The handling of form determines the manner in which this building is done. It may be done in such a way as to produce a great work of art or a poor one, just as building materials may be combined to produce a Taj Mahal or a shack. The important thing, then, in our consideration of form is to find some principles behind the successful building of musical structure—some guiding criteria which will allow us to judge form and acquire a deeper understanding.

It should be said, before going further, that we are concerning ourselves with more complex kinds of music, the longer and more involved types of musical composition. Most shorter compositions—popular songs, hymns, folk songs—depend much less upon form for their value. In such pieces, the melody, rhythm, or words, are the most important things in achieving the desired effect. The longer work must employ formal principles more carefully because it is trying to relate a larger number of musical events.

Form can best be approached by considering the formal problems faced by the composer. The composer is first and foremost trying to achieve a formal structure which is a complete realization of the possibilities inherent in his thematic material. He begins with a musical idea—a melody, a rhythm, a harmonic progression, or any of an endless number of possible things. Each of these thematic ideas has within it many possibilities for development. As the composer works with the material, his goal is to allow that material to grow in a natural way, to realize its inherent potential in the same way that a seed grows into a tree or a flower. He wants the thematic material to work itself out until its full nature has been revealed and until the final form has an organic quality—a quality of seeming to have grown, rather than of having been constructed. We shall listen to a composition which has achieved this objective in a highly successful way:

BEETHOVEN: *Symphony No. 5, Opus 67*, First Movement

Beethoven began with a sparse thematic figure consisting of only four tones, which is the germinal idea for an entire movement. There is hardly a point in the movement where that theme is not being played in some form. The entire movement is the metamorphosis of that initial four-tone figure. After the piece is finished, it is inconceivable that it could have been otherwise. It has achieved a sense of rightness. It has achieved organic form. This is the ultimate aim of the composer: this sense of organism, this rightness, this seeming inevitability.

Unity and Variety

Some components of form are readily accessible to understanding and analysis, for example the concept of **unity** and **variety**. Unity is essential. A piece must seem to hold together and present itself in a coherent fashion. All the thematic material must be compatible, must fit together in a unified way. Still, variety must be attained within this requirement. A composition must not be allowed to become dull. These two formal requirements are often found to be at cross purposes. The most unified piece imaginable would seem to be one which consisted of a single theme, but this could prove to be rather dull if it lasted for very long. The greatest imaginable variety would be found in a piece containing many diverse themes and no repetition. But obviously this piece would not hang together very well. Unity and variety can be seen to present a problem of reconciliation. This is the most basic problem of musical form.

Let us explore some ways in which unity and variety can be achieved. The basic principle is this: Unity is attained primarily through **repetition**; variety is achieved primarily through **contrast**. This can be done in several ways. For a simple example, consider the tune, *America*:

Ex. 8.1

This song consists of two parts, using contrasting melodic ideas. The first six measure section ends with the words, "Of Thee I sing." The second section begins with, "Land where my fathers died" and continues to the end. In a piece this short, the amount of variety needed, or tolerable, is small. It is achieved by using different melodic ideas for the two sections. Unity is gained by seeing to it that the two themes do not contrast too much, that they are similar in nature. In fact, had the difference not been pointed out, it might not have been recognized as a difference at all. This is an illustration of two part, or binary, form, often referred to as AB form. A represents the first melodic idea and B the second. The piece consists of two sections of different, but closely related, melodic material.

For a different manner of solving the unity-variety dilemma, we can cite another short example, *Drink To Me Only With Thine Eyes*:

Ex. 8.2

The song begins with a repeated melodic idea which continues for the period of sixteen triple beat groups. Then at the words "The thirst that from the soul doth rise" a new melody is heard. This continues for eight beat groups after which the original melody returns. The principle involved here is quite different from that of the previous example. Here the second melody is very different from the first, and after the departure from the first melody and the statement of the second, the first melody returns. This song could be diagrammed A A B A. The principle is that of the statement of a theme, departure, and return.

Variety is obtained by the use of the different second section; unity is achieved by the return of the first. This three part, or ternary, form is very important in small works, and the ternary principle is even frequently used as the basis of large and complex forms. This principle holds true even though the first A section is repeated. The immediate repetition of a section does not alter or add to the form.

The unity-variety problem is easier to solve in short compositions than in pieces of greater length. Still, even in longer works, the basic techniques of repetition and contrast are the keys to success. To illustrate this, we turn to two examples of long compositions which have treated the problem in different ways.

RAVEL: *Bolero*

This is a composition which demonstrates a unique way of resolving the problems of unity and variety. The one long theme of the composition is binary, consisting of two closely related sections.

Ex. 8.3

The theme is repeated again and again without any significant alteration. Variety is attained in two ways. First, the instrumentation is changed with each repetition of the theme. Second, the piece becomes constantly louder as the theme is repeated. Third, after almost fifteen minutes of hearing the repetitions of the melody in the same tonality, a sudden shift to a higher tonal center brings the composition to a resounding climax. This achieves variety for the form, and at the same time is largely responsible for the effect which the composer wished to create—that of an incessant crescendo of the same melodic material. Here is a second example:

MUSSORGSKY: *Pictures at an Exhibition*

You will recall having heard this piece, in two versions, in Chapter Three. Each section is different, using very different thematic material. Such a piece could easily become disconnected, could display excessive variety at the expense of unity. You will recognize immediately that this is the reverse problem from the one faced by Ravel in the previous example. Mussorgsky solved the problem through an ingenious use of repetition. The first section of the piece, called *Promenade*, is played between many of the other sections.

Ex. 8.4

This is to represent the strolling from one picture in the gallery to the next. It is interesting to note that these repetitions are never exact, but each is slightly varied in some way. This enhances the variety of the piece without in any way sacrificing unity.

These examples should be sufficient to illustrate the nature of the unity-variety problem and to give a brief look at the way repetition and contrast are used in the solution. The other great goal of form, that of producing a sense of growth in a natural fashion, is perhaps less clear. We shall address that problem further. First, however, we need to examine some of the technical means which a composer may use to seek such organic structure.

THEMATIC PROCESSES: VARIATION AND DEVELOPMENT

We have been concerning ourselves with the basic problems of form—the ultimate problem of organic growth and the component problems of unity and variety. We have seen how the simplest and most basic tools used in the solution of these problems are repetition and contrast. These are the most elementary thematic processes, processes through which the composer shapes his thematic material into what he hopes will be an organic form, one which contains both unity and variety. Despite the usefulness of these processes, the composer would find himself severely handicapped if he were limited to them alone.

There are two reasons for this. First, there would be a limitation upon the length which a composition could attain. With only repetition and contrast available, the amount of variety would be restricted, and this could result in boredom if the composition became very long. The second limitation would be the restriction of the creativity of the composer. Even though he may be gifted in the handling of rhythms, able to write memorable and moving melodies, and capable in any of a number of different skills, the simple techniques of repetition and contrast are not enough if he wishes to build a larger musical structure. He must be able to allow his themes to grow until they attain that sense of organism which we have identified as the goal of most extended music. Thematic processes are needed which allow for more complex formal treatment.

Although the ways in which themes may be treated are practically unlimited, they can be reduced to two fundamental processes in addition to repetition and contrast which we have already discussed. These are variation and development. It is through the many techniques included in these categories that the more complex forms are built.

Variation

*

The term variation is almost self-explanatory. It is a way of presenting a theme in a version different in some way from the original. This allows for more variety than simple repetition without using completely new thematic material. This also contributes to the unity of the piece, by retaining the original theme, although in a different guise. As an example of variation, let us hear the following composition:

BEETHOVEN: *Sonata in G, Opus 14, No. 2*, Second Movement

This movement consists of a theme and three variations. The theme is not one simple melodic idea, but rather is a small ABA form in its own right. Each variation is also a small ABA form, retaining the form of the original theme. As you listen, you will find it easy to recognize each variation as it is played. This, in itself, will give you a good aural definition of variation. And an aural definition is better than a verbal one. Nevertheless, we shall attempt a description of each variation to illustrate some possibilities inherent in the technique.

In the original theme, the melody is presented in the highest voice, with the other voices playing accompanying lines.

Ex. 9.1

The first variation presents two fundamental changes.

Ex. 9.2

The melody is heard in a middle rather than in the topmost voice, and the highest voice presents a counter-melody. These two changes produce an effect quite different from the original, while retaining recognizable relationships to it.

In the second variation the melody is given to the top voice.

Ex. 9.3

Again, however, two changes are made. The rhythm is altered so that the melody notes are always presented on the second half of each beat. Also, the accompanying voices are changed.

This is most noticeable in the lowest line, which plays a more important role than in the original.

The third variation is more complex.

Ex. 9.4

The melody is hidden in the middle of the very rapidly executed notes in the upper voice. The bass again plays a prominent role, being assigned an important countermelody.

The catalog of techniques a composer may use to vary a theme is practically endless. These three variations suggest several. The basic variables are, of course, rhythm, melody, and harmony. These may be varied in any combinations. The only limitations are those imposed by the composer's imagination.

There is a basic principle which governs the writing of variations. That principle is this: In writing a variation, enough of the character of the original theme must be retained to allow for easy recognition, and enough must be changed to make certain the variation is not mistaken for a simple repetition of the theme. The example just heard was successful in this regard, striking an almost perfect balance between the two requirements.

Although generalizations are dangerous and absolutes are non-existent, it is fairly safe to say that in most cases a variation is apt to retain the phrase structure of the original theme. For example, the theme of the movement just heard might be diagrammed: A BA BA. Each of the variations retains the same modified ABA form. This is an important part of our guideline concerning retention of some of the character of the original theme.

It is also fairly safe to say that if one or two musical elements are changed, the other main elements will be retained. For example, if there is a severe rhythmic change, the harmony will probably not be varied. This is, of course, up to the composer. He must judge just how many things about a theme can be varied simultaneously without destroying its identity. To see how three different composers made three different judgments, let us hear the following examples.

IVES: *Variations on America*

BRAHMS: *Variations on a theme of Haydn, Opus 56a*

ELGAR: *Enigma Variations, Opus 36*

The Ives variations are very easy to hear, not only because the theme upon which they are based is familar, but because Ives is careful to retain much of the character of the original theme in each of the variations. The Brahms variations are a bit more complex. While Brahms retains the original phrase structure in each of the variations and several of them are very closely related to the original, many are much farther removed. That is to say, many of them vary several musical elements at once, causing the variation to relate less directly to the original theme. In the Elgar variations, the task is more difficult for the listener. In the first place, the theme is less distinctive and less easy to identify. But, more importantly, the variations are farther removed from the original theme. They alter more of the musical elements simultaneously.

This discussion and a hearing of the examples will give some insight into what is meant by variation and suggest how its use can add variety. Now let us turn to a discussion of development and see how it differs from variation.

Development

This is related to variation, but also very different in many respects. To give us a starting point, we turn to a familiar example:

MOZART: *Symphony No. 40 in G Minor,* First movement

The first theme of this movement is quite distinctive.

Ex. 9.5

This makes it useful for our task of following the theme throughout the movement, no matter in what changed form it may appear. This was our objective in listening to the variations of the last group of examples, but there is a difference here—and that difference will illustrate the technique of development, as contrasted with variation.

We begin with consideration of the nature of the theme. You will notice that it is not one long, flowing melody, but rather is suitable for subdivision into small parts. The first three notes of the theme constitute such a subdivision. Such small units of a theme are known as motives. And it is the use of such motives that characterizes development. As you listen to the movement, you will not hear variations of the complete theme, as you did in the previous examples. Rather, you will hear that small, three-note motive used in a great variety of ways. In fact, you will find that the motive has become thematic material which is used in quite free composition. This illustrates the main difference between variation and development. While variation is the changing of an entire theme, usually retaining the original form, development is the free use of small motives taken from the theme.

The example just heard was a very simple illustration of the use of development based upon one short motive taken from one theme. If a theme were constructed from which several motives could be extracted, if more than one such theme were used, or if the composer wished to take more time to develop the themes, the possibilities would be greatly magnified. Let us consider another example:

BEETHOVEN: *Symphony No. 3, Opus 55*, Fourth Movement

After an introductory section, the movement begins with its main thematic material. The first theme is one which is easily divisible into motives.

Ex. 9.6

The second theme is more flowing and lyric than the first, but is also capable of division.

Ex. 9.7

The development of these themes is complex, but nevertheless some interesting features may be pointed out. For one, the development is mainly of the first theme, or to put it more accurately, of the first four notes of the theme. But in this movement, the composer makes a much longer development and does many different things in his handling of the motive. Also, he sometimes superimposes parts of the second theme over the material he is developing from the first. He is making very free and inventive use of the motives from his original themes. He is trying to allow that material to grow in a way which will seem inevitable and right. The twelve sections of the movement may be diagrammed as follows:

1. *Introduction*	2. *Theme I*	3. *Theme I, Variation I*
4. *Theme I, Variation 2*	5. *Theme II*	6. *Fugal Episode, Based on Theme I*
7. *Theme II, Variation 1*	8. *Theme I, Variation 3*	9. *Theme II, Used as Transition*
10. *Fugal Episode, Inversion of Theme I, Theme II counter-melody*	11. *Theme II, Variation 2*	12. *Coda, Same melodic material used in Introduction*

Ex. 9.8

Perhaps the best example of development which might be cited is the first movement of the *Beethoven Symphony No. 5*, which we heard in the previous chapter. In that movement the first theme is constructed entirely from the initial four-tone motive, with its distinctive rhythmic pattern. The entire movement is then developed from that motive, with the lyrical second theme playing only a minor role.

These two thematic processes, variation and development, along with the simpler ones of repetition and contrast, are the basic tools which a composer has at his disposal for building musical form. The search for unity, variety, and organic growth are the guiding principles which govern the ways in which he will employ these tools. As composers have tried throughout the history of music to achieve these goals, certain patterns have emerged. These patterns have become more or less standardized in the organization of form in music.

SINGLE MOVEMENT INSTRUMENTAL FORMS

As many generations of composers have attempted to solve the problems of form, certain successful designs have emerged and become, to a degree, standardized. These forms provide guidance to the composer by giving him a starting point and a general direction. In the hands of an imaginative composer this is all they do. This is an important point, for it is easy to get the idea that these forms are rigid molds, restricting the composer and imposing limits upon his imagination. These forms serve only as general guides, within which the creative imagination is given great freedom.

It should be remembered that these techniques have evolved as successful ways of achieving good form; they were not simply invented and given as arbitrary laws. In actual practice it is difficult to find examples which follow the typical or "textbook" forms to the letter. Composers are freer and more imaginative than that. They follow not only the outlines of the form in which the music is cast, but also the direction indicated by the thematic material.

In our study it is necessary to make a division between the forms of instrumental and of vocal music. We shall further divide our discussion of instrumental forms into two parts: forms used for single movements and multi-movement forms. In this chapter we shall be concerned with the former.

Two Part Form

*

We have already discussed the basic principles of two part and three part form and have heard examples from the repertory of simple traditional songs. These ideas can also be applied to forms suitable for compositions of larger scope. Here is an example of two part form:

COUPERIN: *Les Nonetes*

Almost any of the works of Couperin would serve as well, since nearly all use two part form. This one is a particularly clear example. In the printed score of this piece, the two parts are identified and even given different names: "Les Blondes" for the first section and "Les Brunes" for the second. The two parts are easy to identify aurally because the second is in a different key. All the things previously said about two part form apply to this piece. The second section is much like the first in character, just as was the case in *America*. The form is too short to allow for much variety, but it is long enough that the change of key in the second section does not jar the ear nor seem misplaced. It is obvious that two part form, even in this more extended piece, must adhere to a minimum of thematic variety in order to hold together aurally. Let us hear a still more advanced use of two part form:

SCARLATTI: *Sonata in C, Longo 282*

As was the case with Couperin, practically any Scarlatti sonata would serve, because all are in two part form. This is a much longer piece than the Couperin example, and the greater length makes possible more variety. For one thing, Scarlatti is able to change keys and cover more tonal territory. But the basic principle of two part form still holds, even in this long composition: all the thematic material is closely related. Variety is limited in a search for unity. In the sonatas of Scarlatti, we see the two part form stretched to its limits. It would not be suitable for pieces much longer than this example.

Three Part Form

*

As was the case with two part form, the simple three part form which we heard in *Drink To Me Only With Thine Eyes* may be used in more extended compositions. Here is an example:

SCHUMANN: *Album for the Young*, Soldiers' March

Ex. 10.1

The two themes are quite similar and entirely compatible. Rhythmically they are almost identical, but the melody of the B theme is less detached, with quarter-notes replacing the eighth-notes followed by eighth-rests.

This piece does not follow the strict A B A pattern which we have discussed previously in connection with three part form. It can be more accurately diagrammed as follows:

AA BA′ BA′

It is, in fact, an A B A with the last two sections repeated. This is not unusual. Although the general outline is A B A, this regular pattern can be varied in a number of ways without losing its identity. Consider the following examples:

SCHUMANN: *Scenes from Childhood*, From Foreign Lands

SCHUMANN: *Scenes from Childhood*, Träumerei

These two pieces illustrate other variations of the basic three part form. The first example could be diagrammed:

AA BA BA

The second piece could be diagrammed the same way, but it is more interesting because of two things. First, the A and B themes are closely related, almost to the point of being identical. Second, the recurrance of the A theme presents it in a slightly different version, one which brings the piece to a more definite close. The result is a close-knit and logical form, a subtle use of the basic A B A.

Although the three part form obviously can take many shapes, the basic construction is always the same: statement—departure—return, involving two themes.

Rondo Forms

*

The principle of statement–departure–return can be extended to include more than two themes. The result is the rondo. It is characterized by a recurring main theme, separated by subordinate themes which may or may not occur more than once. An example of the rondo is to be found in the following composition:

BEETHOVEN: *Sonata Pathétique, Opus 13*, Second Movement

This movement consists of three themes.

Ex. 10.2

It may be diagrammed as follows:

A B A C A

In addition, a short closing section has been added to the basic rondo form. Such a closing section, called a coda, is a common device which is employed at the end of many forms.

In a sense, it is not correct to speak of the rondo as a form. More strictly speaking, it is a family of forms all sharing one characteristic: the recurrance of one main theme separated by sub-themes. Other rondo forms might be diagrammed:

A B A C A D A

A B A C A B A

There is hardly any end to the variety of rondo forms, but all may be recognized by the constantly recurring main theme. It should be pointed out that these repetitions need not be exact. They need only be recognizable. In the example just heard, the main theme, although appearing three times, is never repeated exactly. In the second playing, it is only half as long as in the first. In the third, it is accompanied by a different rhythmic figure.

Ex. 10.3

Still it is easily recognizable, making the rondo form intelligible to the ear.

Minuet and Trio

*

The minuet and trio is an expansion of the three part form. It may be diagrammed as follows:

A	B	A
Minuet	Trio	Minuet

The two sections are usually constructed to present a distinct contrast, making easy the task of the ear in distinguishing them. Here is an example:

MOZART: *Symphony No. 40 in G Minor*, Third Movement

There is little difficulty in locating the beginnings of the two sections, since they contrast so vividly.

Ex. 10.4

It should be evident from this hearing that this is a great expansion of the simple three part form. In the minuet and trio, each of the sections is, in itself, a smaller sectional form:

A	B	A
aa ba ba	cc dc dc	a ba

In a sense, the name minuet and trio may be misleading, for this form is often used for pieces which are in no sense minuets. The form is not restricted to employing the triple meter, fast tempo, and dignity of theme that are required of the dance known as the minuet. It is used also for the scherzo, and for other types of music as well. For example, most Sousa marches are written in this form.

Theme and Variations

*

The name of this form is its best description. It consists simply of a theme followed by any number of variations on that theme. The theme itself is usually a small two part or three part form, and the variations almost invariably retain that same form. As an illustration, we turn to an example already introduced in Chapter 9.

BEETHOVEN: *Sonata in G, Opus 14, No. 2*, Second Movement

We analyzed this movement in chapter nine, but some additional comments are in order. The theme is a small three part form, and each of the variations follows the same form. After the second variation there is some additional material which serves as a transition to variation three. The only reason for the inclusion of this transition is to add variety. For the same reason a coda is added at the end. The use of such material demonstrates that, despite the restrictions of the theme and variations form, the composer is given a great deal of freedom. The imagination is given free reign not only in the composition of the variations themselves, but also in the use of additional material such as the transition and coda we have heard in this illustration.

The Passacaglia

*

The passacaglia also is based upon the technique of variation, but it is a special use of that technique and is quite different from the theme and variations form. To understand the passacaglia, we must investigate a device known as ground bass or *basso ostinato.* Here is an illustration:

PURCELL: *Dido and Aeneas*, Lament

After an introductory section, called a recitative, which ends with the words, "Death is now a welcome guest," the orchestra plays a brief introduction to the aria. This introduction consists of only ten notes, played entirely in the bass line, with the voice entering on the tenth note.

1 2 3 4 5 6 7 8 9
When I am laid, am laid in
10
earth, may my wrongs cre - ate

Ex. 10.5

If you listen carefully, you will hear that same bass line repeated again and again throughout the entire piece. This incessant repetition of the same bass line is known as a ground bass or basso ostinato, a common device for giving unity to a composition. The price the composer is likely to pay, however, is boredom for the audience. Such constant repetition of a short section can soon become dull or annoying. The answer is to write the upper voices in a way which provides constant variety. The result is the passacaglia, which is, in effect, a set of variations over a ground bass. Here is an example:

BACH: *Passacaglia in C Minor*

A ground bass, consisting of fifteen notes, is clearly stated.

Ex. 10.6

With its second statement, the upper voices begin their variations, which continue unbroken until the end of the piece. As with all great composers, Bach finds ways of imposing his own originality upon the form. In several places the ground bass figure is played in voices other than the lowest, and sometimes is even subjected to variation.

The Fugue

*

The fugue is an advanced use of polyphonic texture. It is always written for a specific number of voices, or musical lines, and is therefore referred to as a three-voiced fugue, a four-voiced fugue, or whatever is appropriate to the individual piece. It is usually based upon one theme, known as a **subject**. The beginning section is known as the **exposition**, which consists of the subject being presented by each voice, in turn, in strict imitation. After the exposition is ended, the composer may continue the piece by passing the subject from voice to voice, as in the exposition, or he may introduce sections, known as **episodes**, of new melodic material. As a rule, he will do both, alternating episodes with statements of the subject.

The fugue is easily recognized by the extensive use of imitation. The basic technique, of course, is similar to that used in the round, or canon, such as *Row, Row, Row Your Boat*. The fugue, however, is more free and allows for more creative composition. Here is a famous example of the fugue:

BACH: *"Little" Fugue in G Minor*

Sonata-Allegro Form

*

Without doubt, this is the most important single movement

form. Its importance will become more apparent as we study the multi-movement forms and as we deal later with more detailed analysis. Sonata-Allegro is a large version of the basic A B A form. The three parts are known as the exposition, the development, and the recapitulation. Diagrammed, it would look like this:

A	B	A
Exposition	Development	Recapitulation

The names of the three sections describe their functions. The exposition sets forth, or exposes, the thematic material upon which the movement will be based; the development uses that material in free composition; the recapitulation restates the thematic material. This simple description requires some amplification, so we should examine each of the three sections in a bit more detail.

The **exposition** consists of at least two themes of contrasting characters and tonalities. The word "theme" is a little misleading, perhaps, since it leaves the impression of a single melodic idea. Actually, the themes may be fairly complex small forms containing several melodic ideas. In every case, however, all the melodic material within a single theme is closely related and seems to the ear to belong together.

In the classic sonata-allegro, the first theme is usually energetic in nature and is always in the tonic key. The second theme is ordinarily more lyrical in character and is in a closely related key. Often there is a third theme, or closing theme, which is usually in a closely related key. The key relationships play an important role in the earlier sonata-allegro movements, but lose their centrality in the sonata-allegro forms of the middle and later nineteenth century.

The **development** section is based upon material presented in the exposition and sometimes upon new material introduced in the development itself. There is no prescribed form. Here the composer exercises his originality to its highest degree. The themes are developed in a great variety of ways and are presented in many different keys, some of them foreign, before giving way to the more fixed form of the recapitulation.

The **recapitulation** reintroduces the themes heard in the exposition, but this time they are all in the tonic key. This re-establishes the key center, or tonality, and makes possible a more final feeling at the end of the movement, something which is often needed after the foreign excursions taken during the development. This description will have more meaning if we relate it to an example:

MOZART: *Symphony No. 40 in G Minor*, First Movement

The movement begins with a vigorous first theme, as is typical of the form.

Ex. 10.7

The lyricism of the second theme contrasts vividly, making it easy to identify. Also, while the first theme is played by the strings, the second theme features the woodwinds.

Ex. 10.8

The development section is quite short and is based entirely upon the first theme, mostly upon the first three-note motive. The recapitulation may be identified by the return of the first theme in its original form.

More than any other form, the sonata-allegro provides a useful framework for a composition without imposing restrictions upon a composer's creativity. It is suitable for even the most extended compositions as well as for those of more modest proportions. This adaptability has made it the form which is probably the most popular of all those developed over the past two hundred years.

The forms discussed in this chapter are by no means the only ones which history has given us. They are, however, major ones and those which most often appear as movements of more extended works. It is to a study of these longer, compound forms that we now turn.

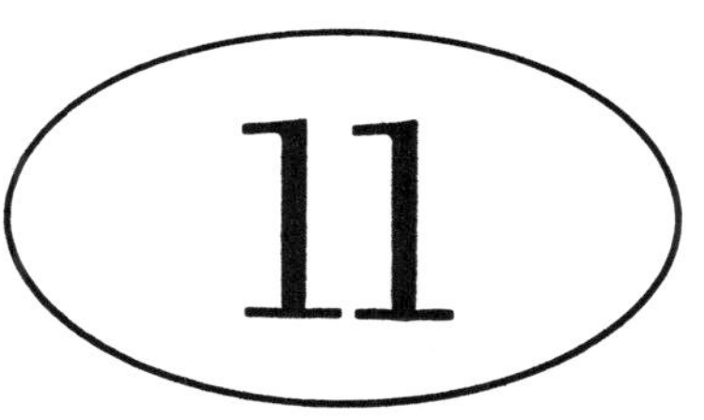

MULTI-MOVEMENT INSTRUMENTAL FORMS

MOST

of the major works of instrumental music have been conceived in terms too large to be contained within the single movement forms. These compositions have used more extensive forms composed of several separate but related movements. In this chapter we turn to a brief examination of those forms most frequently encountered.

The Sonata

*

The sonata is probably the most influential form ever devised, not only because it has been the foundation for so many major works, but also because it is the basis for such other compound forms as the symphony, the concerto, and the string quartet. As with all multi-movement forms, the sonata exists in many variations. It is not possible to describe a "typical" sonata form, even to the extent to which we could describe the single-movement forms. We can, however, make some very general comments about the sonata and describe its features in broad terms.

The sonata usually consists of three or four movements, related by key and tempo. Without these relationships the sonata would be no more than a collection of individual, shorter pieces. They act as a cohesive force holding the movements together in a larger unity. In most instances, the first movement is in sonata-allegro form. The other movements may be in any form chosen by the composer. To make our discussion clearer and more concrete, let us hear an example:

BEETHOVEN: *Sonata Pathétique in C Minor, Opus 13*

This three-movement sonata illustrates the typical features of the form. The first movement is sonata-allegro. It differs from the sonata-allegro movements previously studied in that it begins with a slow introduction before the main themes of the exposition are played. This is a common feature found in many sonata-allegro movements. The second and third movements are both in rondo form.

The tempo and key relationships referred to earlier are clearly illustrated here. The first movement is fast, the second slow, and the third fast. Obviously the composer is trying to achieve unity and variety over the entire work as well as within each movement. This fast–slow–fast tempo scheme is effective in this attempt. Variety is achieved by the alternating tempi; unity is encouraged by the recurrance of a fast tempo after the slow digression. In a sense this is a ternary, A B A pattern applied to the tempo scheme of the three movements.

The same thing can be said of the tonalities of the movements. The first is in c minor, the second in A-flat Major, and the third in c minor, again a kind of A B A applied to the key relationships. Since the sonata begins and ends in c minor, this is said to be the tonic key of the composition. The A-flat Major movement is in a closely related key. The parallel between this inter-movement use of key relationships and the employment of such relationships in the exposition of the sonata-allegro is worth noting. Each of these uses has the same purpose: to achieve variety through the use of different key centers, but to preserve unity by keeping the keys closely related.

The sonata is usually written for a solo instrument or for solo instrument with piano. When the form is employed for performance by other media, it takes on other names. We turn now to an examination of some of these other uses of the sonata form.

The Symphony

*

A symphony is a sonata for orchestra. The general description of the sonata applies to the symphony as well. To illustrate the point we turn to a now familiar example:

MOZART: *Symphony No. 40 in G Minor, K.550*

This symphony is in four movements. The first, second, and fourth movements are in sonata-allegro form; the third is a minuet and trio. This use of the minuet and trio for the third movement of a four-movement symphony was standard in the late eighteenth century. The relationship of the movements by tempo, as in the Beethoven sonata, is also present in this symphony. Fast–slow–fast–very fast is the pattern employed here. The relationship by key is also present. The keys of the four movements are as follows:

First Movement: g minor
Second Movement: E–flat Major
Third Movement: g minor–G Major–g minor
Fourth Movement: g minor

The key scheme is limited to the tonic, g minor, and two closely related keys: G Major and E-flat Major. This relationship of the movements by tempo and key is common to all varieties of the sonata.

The Concerto

*

The concerto is a sonata for solo instrument and orchestra. The special use of a solo instrument makes necessary certain alterations in the basic form. Here is an illustration:

MOZART: *Piano Concerto No. 3 in E-flat, K.107*

This is an early Mozart concerto and is typical in that it contains only two movements. Normally the classical concerto consists of three movements, and sometimes four. This composition is, however, a particularly clear example of the basic differences between the concerto and the other varieties of the sonata. These differences may be heard in the first movement, which varies from the typical sonata-allegro. The orchestra first plays the thematic material, and then it is repeated by the solo instrument. This is often referred to as a double exposition, although this term overstates the case. The themes are seldom played in their entirety by the orchestra and solo instrument in turn. Still, the presence of the solo instrument seems to necessitate a longer and more complex exposition in this form.

A second difference is illustrated near the end of the movement, when the orchestra stops and the solo instrument plays a free and improvisatory section, known as a *cadenza.* Originally cadenzas were not written out, but were improvised on the spot by the soloist. In later concertos the composer actually wrote out the cadenzas, and in most instances dispensed with the double exposition. As examples of more mature concertos, the following are suggested:

BEETHOVEN: *Piano Concerto No. 4 in G, Opus 58*

TCHAIKOVSKY: *Violin Concerto in D*, First Movement

BRAHMS: *Piano Concerto No. 1 in D Minor, Opus 15*

The String Quartet

A sonata for two violins, viola, and cello is known as a string quartet. Quartets are usually in four movements and follow the same outline as the symphony. Here is an example:

BEETHOVEN: *Quartet No. 1, Opus 18, No. 1*

The four movements are, as was seen in the sonata and the symphony, related by tempo and key. The third movement is a scherzo, a fast dance using minuet and trio form. This quartet is typical of the form in general and illustrates the nearly complete identity with the "typical" sonata form.

Other Uses of the Sonata Form

*

The analyses presented here should be sufficient to prove the point: the sonata form is the parent of a wide variety of important compound forms, the names of which are dependent upon the performing media for which they are intended. This principle can be extended to a bewildering array of compositional types. A quintet is a sonata for five instruments; a trio is a sonata for three instruments; the applications of the basic idea are endless. Once the basic sonata is understood, the door is open for the understanding of all its derivatives.

The Concerto Grosso

*

Although having a similar name, the concerto grosso is quite different from the concerto. The concerto, as defined before, is a creation of the late eighteenth and nineteenth centuries and is a variety of the sonata. The concerto grosso was developed in the late seventeenth and early eighteenth centuries and has nothing at all to do with the sonata.

The concerto grosso is a multi-movement composition for orchestra and a smaller instrumental group. As a rule the orchestra contains only strings; the small group, called the *concertino*, may consist of any number or type of instruments. Most often, the concerto grosso contains three movements. As with the other compound forms we have discussed, these are related by tempo and key. There is, however, no set form for any of the movements. They usually are sectional in nature, with no set arrangement of the sections. The characteristic sound of the concerto grosso is attained through the dialogue between the two basic textures–the thin texture of the *concertino* and the thicker one of the orchestra, or *ripieno*. Here is a famous example:

BACH: *Brandenburg Concerto No. 5*

The piece is in three movements with the characteristic arrangement of fast–slow–fast. The orchestra is composed of strings. The concertino consists of harpsichord, flute, and violin. Characteristic of many examples of the form is the second movement which is played entirely by the concertino. While dating from more than two hundred years ago, this form has been revived and used by many modern composers.

The Suite

*

This is a title which is used to describe two very different types of composition. In the Baroque period it meant a collection of court dances. Usually included were an allemande, a courante, a saraband, a gigue, and sometimes other dances. This purely concert music was an outgrowth of music which has actually been used to accompany dancing. Here is a well known example:

HANDEL: *Suite No. 1 in B-flat*

In later periods the term suite has another meaning which is altogether different from the one discussed above. It is used to refer to a set of instrumental excerpts from a large dramatic form such as an opera or a ballet. More broadly, it may refer to any collection of pieces intended to be played together. Probably the most famous such piece is Tchaikovsky's suite drawn from the ballet, *The Nutcracker.* There is an abundance of famous examples found in the concert literature: Bizet's *L'Arlesienne Suites,* the suites from Stravinsky's ballets, and many others. The following example is typical of the modern suite:

RAVEL: *Daphnis et Chloé*, Suite No. 2

Free Forms

*

The number of forms which could be described under this heading is staggering. We shall consider only two: the overture and the symphonic poem. We must, however, consider a problem which we have not mentioned before—the distinction between so-called absolute music and program music.

To this point we have been concerned only with absolute music—music which makes no claim to any "meaning" outside itself. Absolute music is simply intended to be enjoyed on its own terms. One does not need ask what the Mozart *Symphony No. 40* means. Its meaning is inherent in the music itself. There is a category of music, however, which has other considerations. Such music is called program music, and attempts to tell a story or describe a scene.

You can easily see that this represents an aesthetic problem of considerable proportions. The question of how a piece of music can portray some concrete, extra-musical thing, or if it can do so at all, is one which has filled many volumes and is still unresolved. Leaving that problem to critic and philosopher, we can turn to the music itself. Whether or not we can discern in the music the meanings intended by the composers is less important than our hearing of the music.

Two of the most important forms which have resulted from the production of program music are the program overture and the symphonic poem.

The Overture

Originally an overture was a composition played before an opera or a play. While retaining that meaning, the form has come to be employed independently, usually as a form of program music. Here is an example of the programmatic overture:

TCHAIKOVSKY: *Romeo and Juliet, Fantasy Overture*

In this overture, the composer attempts to tell the story only in the most general terms. This is done by attaching particular narrative significance to each of the main themes. The first, hymn-like melody is supposed to represent the cell of Friar Lawrence.

Ex. 11.1

The vigorous second theme represents the feud between the Montagues and the Capulets.

Ex. 11.2

The third theme symbolizes the love of Romeo and Juliet.

Ex. 11.3

There is no attempt to tell the story in detail. In fact, the thematic treatment follows purely musical logic and does not need the story to justify its existence. Although the listener, if he has prior knowledge of the meaning of the themes, can probably follow the literary idea in a general way, this is not necessary for the enjoyment of the music itself. This is true of all the best program music. The extra-musical idea may enhance the musical experience, but is not a necessary part.

The Symphonic Poem

✻

This is the most important of the program forms. Some symphonic poems attempt to follow a very detailed story line, or program, scene by scene and event by event. They use the program to guide the form, rather than adhering to the formal principles of absolute music as we have discussed them in previous chapters. Such a composition is the following:

STRAUSS: *Tod und Verklärung*

The original program for this piece described a dying man who goes through his last agony recalling the events of a life which has been in many ways a failure. The music describes the death scene and the fantasies imagined by the dying man, and attempts to do so in the most minute detail. In the end, the man dies, only to discover that death has brought him release from a life of pain and has given him the beginning of a transfigured existence.

This type of fanciful story is typical of the romantic movement which gave birth to the program forms. Whether the program is really helpful to the understanding of the music depends, in part, upon the personality and preference of the listener. The music can stand on its own merits.

The forms discussed in this chapter are by no means the only ones found in the concert repertory. But the examples contained here do represent and illustrate the most important and influential major instrumental forms in current use. In the next chapter we turn our attention to the major forms of music for the voice.

THE MAJOR VOCAL FORMS

BEFORE *considering the major forms of vocal music, we must make clear a fundamental difference between vocal and instrumental composition. This goes beyond the technical and extends to stylistic and aesthetic differences as well. The style of vocal music is influenced by both the possibilities and the limitations of the human voice. Let us first consider the limitations, since these influence style in the most direct way.*

The most obvious limitation of the human voice is its range. The average untrained voice has a range of only about an octave and a half. The professionally trained voice usually covers two octaves, but rarely much more. This range is far shorter than most instruments and very much less than such instruments as the piano. This limitation of the single voice is in turn imposed upon the range of the vocal ensemble. The three and one half octave range of a chorus, from the lowest bass to the highest soprano voice, is hardly comparable to the vast range of the orchestra, from the contrabassoon to the piccolo.

Not only is the vocal ensemble limited in range, but also in variety of tone color. The orchestra is replete with colors and with color combinations. The four families of instruments are fundamentally different in sound, the individual instruments differ within each family, and the combinations available among the instruments are practically endless. The four voice types—soprano, alto, tenor, and bass—differ much less and make fewer combinations possible.

A third limitation of the voice is one of agility. Many instruments, such as the violin, the flute, and the clarinet, are capable of playing extremely rapid and complex lines. Although many trained singers can sing rapid, florid passages, none can approach the agility of these instruments. Further, when voices are brought together into an ensemble, the capability of florid performance is markedly lowered. This is much less true of instrumental ensembles. So the composer who writes for voice, particularly vocal ensemble, is severely limited in the type of melody he can use. It must be of smaller range and of much simpler construction than it could be if it were intended for instrumental performance.

These limitations are offset to a great degree by some remarkable capabilities not possessed by instruments. The most obvious of these is the ability to use language. Another is the particular ability of the voice to change color in very subtle ways to suit the demands of the music. These very possibilities, however, put vocal music in a completely different category from music for instruments. In fact, music for the voice is usually based upon a different aesthetic and pursues different goals than instrumental music.

In the last chapter we distinguished between absolute music and program music. We found that most instrumental music comes under the former category; it does not concern itself with external meaning. The composer is guided by the nature of his themes and by certain principles of form. Even when instrumental music pretends to external connotations, the formal principles are the same. A successful piece of instrumental program music can stand on its own merits; the external program is not necessary for enjoyment. But with vocal music the situation is different. Practically all vocal compositions can be considered program music. They are based upon words, and the words are what the music is all about. The composer, while still observing the basic principles of form, is primarily concerned with expressing the meaning of the words. He is guided by them, and if he is successful, he intensifies their meaning through his use of music. This puts vocal music into a unique category and makes necessary a somewhat different set of criteria for the critical listener. To illustrate this, let us hear an example:

SCHUBERT: *Erlkoenig*

The poem, by Goethe, tells the story of a father riding through the night with his son. As they ride, the son tells the father that they are being pursued by the Erl-King. The father assures the son that what he sees and hears amounts only to the mist, the willows in the moonlight, and the rustling of leaves. Here is the German poem and an English translation of the complete text:

Wer reitet so spät durch Nacht und Wind?
Es ist der Vater mit seinem Kind;
Er hat den Knaben wohl in dem Arm,
Er fasst ihn sicher, er hält ihn warm.

NARRATOR:
Who rides so late in night and wind?
It is a father and his son.
He has the boy in his arms
And holds him tightly to keep him warm.

Mein Sohn, was birgst du so bang dein Gesicht?

FATHER:
"My son, why make such an anxious face?"

Siehst, Vater, du den Erlkönig nicht?
Den Erlenkönig mit Kron' und Schweif?

SON:
"Oh, father, don't you see the Erlking?
The Erlking with crown and robe."

Mein Sohn, es ist ein Nebelstreif.

FATHER:
"My son, it's only a wisp of fog."

"Du liebes Kind, komm, geh' mit mir!
Gar schöne Spiele spiel' ich mit dir;
Manch' bunte Blumen sind an dem Strand,
Meine Mutter hat manch gülden Gewand."

ERLKING:
"You lovely child, come, go with me,
Such happy games I'll play with you.
Many radiant flowers bloom near my house,
My mother has golden clothes for you."

Mein Vater, mein Vater, und hörest du nicht,
Was Erlenkönig mir leise verspricht?

SON:
"Oh, father, father, do you hear
What the Erlking softly promises me?"

Sei ruhig, bleibe ruhig, mein Kind;
In dürren Blättern säuselt der Wind.

FATHER:

"Be still, be still, my child,
It's only the wind rattling the dead leaves."

"Willst, feiner Knabe, du mit mir geh'n?
Meine Töchter sollen dich warten schön
Meine Töchter führen den nächtlichen Reih'n
Und wiegen und tanzen und singen dich ein,
Sie wiegen und tanzen und singen dich ein."

ERLKING:

"Will you go with me, you wonderful boy?
My daughters will wait on you,
And every night they'll dance with you,
They'll sing and dance and lull you to sleep
They'll sing and dance and lull you to sleep."

Mein Vater, mein Vater, und siehst du nicht dort
Erlkönigs Töchter am düstern Ort?

SON:

"Father, father, you surely must see
Erlking's daughters waiting for me."

Mein Sohn, mein Sohn, ich seh' es genau,
Es scheinen die alten Weiden so grau.

FATHER:

"My son, my son, of course I see;
The waving branches of an old willow tree."

"Ich liebe dich, mich reizt deine schöne Gestalt,
Und bist du nicht willig, so brauch' ich Gewalt."

ERLKING:

"You've got to come, you handsome boy,
And if not freely, I'll take you by force!"

Mein Vater, mein Vater, jetzt fasst er mich an!
Erlkönig hat mir ein Leid's gethan!

SON:

"Father, father, he's caught hold of me!
Erlking is crushing me so!"

Dem Vater grauset's, er reitet geschwind,
Er hält in Armen das ächzenden Kind,
Erreicht den Hof mit Müh und Noth;
In seinem Armen das Kind war todt.

NARRATOR:

The father shudders and gallops his horse.
He holds his moaning child in his arms,
Arrives at the courtyard with fear and dread,
And in his arms, the child . . . was dead.

This is a classic example of the great possibilities of music for the voice. The accompaniment creates the effect of the night ride. The voice line involves four distinct characterizations: the father, the son, the Erl-King, and the narrator. Schubert differentiates between these in very subtle ways. The effect which he tries to attain is that of ever-mounting fear by the father, from an initial uneasiness to a final dread which is consummated by the son's death. This is done by writing the son's lines in such a way that each is at a higher pitch level than the one preceding. The final description of the son's death is then done in a completely straightforward and simple recitative style as the narrator sings: "*In seinem Armen das Kind war todt*" (And in his arms, the child . . . was dead). Listen for the dramatic chords in the last line and the pause before the words, "*war todt.*" The effect is one of irony and stark terror.

There is much more than this involved in the aesthetic of *Erlkoenig*, but this is enough to illustrate the kind of problems and possibilities faced by the composer of music for the voice. It is a different thing in many ways from instrumental music. Consequently, music for voice has taken different forms from those used for instruments. These forms are the concern of this chapter.

The Art Song

*

The song is the shortest and most pervasive of the vocal forms. At the same time, it embraces some of the most profound expressions in the history of music. There is no set form for the song, such as there is for the instrumental forms we have studied. As with all vocal music, the words dictate the structure. There are, however, some general patterns. Of these the most important are the strophic song and the through-composed song. A strophic song sets several stanzas or verses to the same music, often a small AB or ABA form. The through-composed song is just what the name implies: a song which begins, continues, and ends according to the requirements of the words, using new music throughout, rather than repeating the same music for different words. Some examples will help make this clearer.

SCHUBERT: *Heidenroeslein*

This is an example of a strophic song. It consists of three verses. The first tells of a boy discovering a small hedge-rose. The second tells of the rose defending itself from being picked by pricking the boy. The third tells of the boy's picking the rose. Each of the stanzas is set to identical music in this simple but effective song.

This song illustrates a peculiar problem and a peculiar opportunity associated with the strophic song. On the surface, it is difficult to see how one bit of music can meet the expressive needs of different words. But it affords an opportunity to use parallel musical ideas for closely related verbal ideas. The repeated words,

"Roeslein, Roeslein, Roeslein rot,
Roeslein auf dem Heiden."

at the end of each stanza are underscored by the repeated

musical idea. The effect is just what the poem requires. It is inconceivable that this little poem could have been set in other than strophic form. Here, in the setting of a poem by Verlaine, is another example of the strophic song:

HAHN: *L'Heure Exquise*

Below are the French and Exglish texts for *L'Heure Exquise.*

La lune blanche	The silver moon
Luit dans les bois;	Streams in the woods.
De chaque branche	From ev'ry branch
Part une voix	Murmurs a voice
Sous la ramée	Soft as a sigh
O bienaimée.	O, my beloved.
L'étang reflète,	The pool reflects
Profond miroir	Like a dark mirror
La silhouette	The silhouette
Du saule noir	Of the black column
Ou le vent pleure	Where the wind weeps.
Rêvons, c'est l'heure!	Dream on . . . It is the hour!
Un vaste et tendre	A great and tender
Apaisement,	Soulful peace
Semble descendre	Seems to come down
Du firmament	From the heavens
Que l'astre irise.	Like a starry iris.
C'est l'heure exquise.	It is the hour of ecstasy.

Leger et lointain
pp
p
La lu - ne blan - che Luit dans les
bois;
De cha - que - bran - che

Ex. 12.1

Here is an example of a through-composed song:

DEBUSSY: *Le Chevelure*

This is a much more complex poem than the one used for the previous song, and the music is accordingly less straightforward. The only way this poem could have been successfully set is by the use of through-composition. In general, longer and more complex texts are set in this fashion, particularly if the text is narrative in nature. *Erlkoenig* is an excellent example.

In addition to strophic and through-composed songs, many use simple AB and ABA forms. Some even are small rondos. Here are some examples:

Two Part

SCHUBERT: *Der Tod und das Maedchen*

SCHUMANN: *Du bist wie eine Blume*

SCHUMANN: *Jasminenstrauch*

Three Part

COPLAND: *Simple Gifts*

Rondo

SCHUBERT: *Die boese Farbe*

The Song Cycle

*

This is a series of related songs. The text may be a single poem too long for setting in one song, a set of poems intended by the poet to belong together, or a series of related poems chosen by the song composer as having enough affinity for each other to become the text for a large composition. For the purpose of study we turn to a famous example:

SCHUMANN: *Frauenliebe und Leben*

This cycle consists of eight songs based on poems by Adelbert V. Chamisso. It is not a narrative story, but eight lyric poems depicting the climactic points in the life of a woman. These represent the practically universal experience of the typical woman, at least as history has painted her portrait, and therefore have a great power and appeal. The texts are summarized and paraphrased:

1. **Seit itch ihn gesehen**
Since I have seen him, I am blind to all else. Everything else is pale. I no longer wish to share in my sisters' games. Since I have seen him, I believe I am blind.

2. **Er, der herrlichste von Allen**
He, the most glorious of all, how kind and

good. My star; my heaven. Do not hear my quiet plea for your happiness. You must not know me, a lowly maid. Only the most worthy should make you happy. Then I should rejoice even though my heart should break.

3. **Ich kann's nicht fassen, nicht glauben**
I cannot grasp nor believe it. That he should have chosen me from all others. Oh, let me die in this dream, close to his breast. Let me drink blessed death in tears of unending joy.

4. **Du Ring an meinem Finger**
You ring on my finger, my little golden ring, I press you to my lips and my heart. My childhood dream had ended. I found myself alone in unending space. You showed me life's deep and eternal worth. I will live for him alone.

5. **Helft mir, ihr Schwestern**
Help me, sisters, the happy one. Strew flowers before him. I greet you with sadness, as I depart from you with joy.

6. **Suesser Freund**
Sweet friend, you do not understand my

weeping. Let the moist pearls tremble in my eyes. How filled with rapture my heart is. If I only had the words to tell you. Come and put your face on my breast, let me whisper all my happiness. Now you know the tears that I shed. Should you not see them, you beloved man? Here by my bed the cradle will be, where it may conceal my beautiful dream. There will come the morning when the dream awakes, and your likeness will look up at me in laughter.

7. **An meinem Herzen, an meiner Brust**
On my heart, on my breast, happiness is love and love is happiness. Only a mother knows real happiness. You beloved angel, you look at me and smile.

8. **Nun hast du mir den ersten Schmerz getan**
Now you have given me the first hurt. You sleep the sleep of death. The world is empty. I have lived and loved but live no more.

The cycle is couched in very romantic, nineteenth-century words which are, in some measure, strange to our ears. But the combination of text and music powerfully expresses universal feelings which are the subject of the work.

The Opera

*

The art song is the shortest and simplest of the vocal forms. The opera is the longest and most complex. In fact, the opera is the most complex form of all music. It involves drama, music, and pure spectacle, which must be seen to be truly understood.

Briefly put, an opera is a play with the lines sung, rather than spoken. The form dates from the very early seventeenth century, when it emerged from an attempt to re-create the Greek drama. It has gone through many phases of development since that time, and is still influential in the form of the musical play, as well as the opera proper. We will consider two examples of different types:

MOZART: *Don Giovanni*, Opera

This type of work is known as a number opera. This means simply that the work consists of a series of "numbers" or separate pieces which fit together to make up the complete play. These consist of recitatives, or rapidly executed, speech-like sections, which advance the story and add little to the musical value; arias, which are solo songs designed to reveal the inner thoughts of a character; and ensembles, such as trios, quartets, and choruses. On the printed score, each of these sections is printed separately and given an identifying number.

This story is of that famous libertine, Don Juan. The setting is Seville. In the first act we find ourselves in the commandant's courtyard. Don Juan's servant, Leporello, is nervously waiting and complaining, awaiting the Don's emergence from inside, where he is an unknown and uninvited guest. The hour is, in fact, much too late for any guest, invited or not. The Don emerges, struggling with the commandant's daughter, Donna Anna, who has resisted his advances. His identity is not known to her. The commandant enters and tries to stop the Don with his sword. In the struggle, Don Juan kills the commandant. Donna Anna is consoled by Don Ottavio.

In the second scene of Act I, we are in a street early in the morning. Leporello is taking his master to task for being such a rogue when a young lady enters. The Don and Leporello hide as she laments having been loved and deserted. The Don, seeing an opportunity, comes forward to console her, only to find that she is known to him, and that he is in fact the false lover she is disclaiming. The Don flees, leaving her with Leporello, who provides her with the slight consolation that she is only one among hundreds of other ladies.

In scene three, the Don seduces a peasant girl, Zerlina, on her own wedding day. Her betrothed, Masetto, is justifiably enraged. At this point the Don is the target of the hate of many people: Donna Anna, Don Ottavio, Donna Elvira, Zerlina, and Masetto. He is not even greatly admired by Leporello, who has seen too much of the Don's philandering.

In Act II, the Don engages in several other attempted seductions. In an effort to escape some difficulties involved in one of them, he finds himself in a churchyard. There he confronts a statue of the commandment whom he has killed. The statue speaks to the Don. Although frightened, the Don defiantly invites the statue to dinner. He accepts.

As the dinner party is in full swing, the statue enters. Defiantly the Don offers his hand. When he clasps the hand of the statue, the ground begins to tremble and the flames of hell engulf Don Juan. Although having been given many chances to repent, he has arrogantly declined them, and has now paid the price. The opera ends with a rejoicing of all the other major characters in the drama.

Don Giovanni is a comic tragedy or a tragic comedy; choose your own interpretation. The setting captures both moods and the subtleties of their interaction in a way not possible for a spoken play. The music, while great in its own right, is really the servant of the drama.

* * *

A different approach to the opera does not divide the work into separate numbers, but allows the music to form a continuous texture. Although arias can still be identified in many of these works, the separation is less distinct, and usually no recitative is used. Instead, the action is advanced by material of a more melodic nature.

PUCCINI: *La Bohème*, Opera

This is a story of the lives of four young artists and scholars in the Paris of the 1840's. They are Rodolfo, a poet; Schaunard, a musician; Marcello, a painter; and Colline, a philosopher. The story is almost anecdotal in nature, providing glimpses into the lives of these men and their friends, rather than telling a continuous story.

In the first act, the only continuing story element is introduced: the meeting between the men and the young girl, Mimi. It becomes apparent at that time that a love affair is to develop between her and Rodolfo. In the second act, a comic opera in its own right, the young people visit the Cafe Momus. This allows development of the love theme. In the third act Mimi, quite penurious (as are the young men), goes away to live with a rich nobleman for support. In the final act, Mimi returns to Rodolfo. She is ill and wants to be with her lover at the end.

This is a simple story line. The thing which is important is the manner in which Puccini uses the music. We are allowed such intimate glimpses into the lives of these people that we seem to know them personally, a fact which intensifies the final tragedy. All the time, the music underscores this in the subtlest ways. This is done by associating certain themes with characters or situations in the story. A musical illustration will point this out more clearly:

In the last act, Mimi seems to be asleep. All the other characters except Rodolfo leave the room in order not to awaken her. When they are gone, she opens her eyes and sings a little aria. She says she only pretended to sleep in order to be alone with Rodolfo. The little tune to which these words are set had not previously been heard in the entire opera.

Ex. 12.2

In the end, when Rodolfo realizes she is dead, this tune thunders from the full orchestra, providing a chilling and overpoweringly ironic ending. It is thematic treatment such as this that pervades the entire opera, and most other operas that use music in this most effective and dramatic way.

Although opera *per se* has not become an indigenous part of American culture, it does thrive in several ways. Professional opera companies are not plentiful, but the opera productions associated with college music schools and departments are staggering in number, and many are impressive in quality. In addition, the musical show, a very live part of American culture, is derived from opera, and is in fact quite worthy of being called an operatic form.

The Oratorio

The oratorio is often referred to as a sacred opera. While there is an element of truth in this definition, it is not entirely accurate. The oratorio usually, but not always, has a sacred text. It consists, as does the number opera, of solos, duets, trios, choruses, and other ensembles. It does in some sense tell a story. But it is not necessarily a play set to music. Some oratorios are very nearly such. They have characters and tell narrative stories. Mendelssohn's *Elijah* is probably the most famous of these dramatic oratorios. But even *Elijah* could not be called a true opera. The development of the story is not as complete or as dramatic as an opera would require. Also, oratorios are not ordinarily performed with stage sets, costumes, or lighting—things absolutely necessary to opera performances. Some attempts have been made to stage oratorios, but the results have been questionable in most cases.

Many oratorios do not even have this much of a dramatic element, but present their content in a form which could only loosely be called narrative. These oratorios contain material which is closely related to a central theme, but they have no dramatic plot. We shall hear the most famous example of all:

HANDEL: *Messiah*, Oratorio

This work concerns the prophecy, the birth, the crucifixion, of Jesus, and the hope given to Christians by these events. It is in three sections. The first deals with the prophecies surrounding the birth of Christ and with the Nativity. The second deals with the Crucifixion. The third concerns the triumph which the Christian Church feels because of the life of Christ.

This oratorio is not dramatic, nor is it narrative. Its material is, however, presented in a logical sequence in relationship to its central theme.

The Cantata

*

The cantata is similar to the oratorio in some ways. It is usually sacred in character and often consists of an alternation of solos and ensembles. However, it is usually of much smaller scope. Also, the cantata is often set for solo voice, without ensembles. Even when this is the case, the cantata consists of several separate pieces centering around a single theme. We shall hear an example of each type.

BACH: *Ich habe genug*, Cantata

This cantata is for the baritone voice alone. It consists of an aria, followed by a recitative and aria, and then by another recitative and aria. The text concerns the sense of weariness with life and the joy of death for the convinced Christian. Bach was himself certainly one of these, and his music is filled with this theme.

BACH: *Wachet auf*, Cantata

Here we see the cantata in its most developed form. The text concerns the parable of the wise virgins, and calls for all to awake and look for the coming of Christ. This cantata, intended for Advent, is composed of a chorus, a tenor recitative, a soprano and bass duet, a chorale for tenor voice, a bass recitative, a soprano and bass duet, and a final chorus. All the choruses are based upon the final chorale melody:

Ex. 12.3

This illustrates the similarity to the oratorio, but also demonstrates the much smaller scale of the cantata.

The Mass

✽

Since earliest times, the Christian Mass has been set to music. Formerly, these settings were intended for use in actual services. But in the eighteenth and nineteenth centuries, the text of the mass began to be used specifically for concert compositions. Each section of the ordinary of the mass served as the basis for several musical movements of varying types. As in the oratorio and cantata, solos and ensembles were usually alternated. A famous contemporary example is:

KODÀLY: *Missa Brevis*

The understanding of vocal music differs considerably from that of instrumental music. Not only are we concerned with the development of the musical ideas, but also with the relationship of these ideas to the text. The matter is complicated by the fact that many of the texts of some of the greatest vocal compositions are in languages other than English. The question is always whether the pieces should be sung in the original language in order to preserve the most subtle nuances, or whether English translations should be made in order to present the main outlines of the idea at the expense of many subtleties. There is no satisfactory answer to that question. It is a matter of taste. Either way, the heritage of music for the voice is great and worth the considerable effort necessary to hear and understand it.

A PLAN FOR STYLE ANALYSIS

As our study has progressed, we have gone more deeply into the important features of the art of music. Our first acquaintance was with musical elements, the basic building blocks of musical composition. We next considered musical form, the ways in which these elements are combined into a musical work. We are now at the point where we are able to consider music on its highest level, that of style.

In chapter one we defined style as that which differentiates between compositions, between composers, between musical types, and between compositions from different historical periods. All music is related through the use of similar formal principles, but differentiated by stylistic features. Although all music consists of the same elements, these elements may be used in an endless variety of ways. The differences in usage are stylistic.

An understanding of musical style is the main goal of our study, for two reasons. First, style is the most abstract and subjective feature of music. The ability to deal with it is evidence of a growing understanding. Second, it is in being conscious of style that we become mature listeners. All educated listening is, in a sense, an act of conscious or unconscious aural stylistic analysis.

When we listen to music, we can listen in a number of ways. We can listen passively, paying little or no conscious attention to the music. Much listening is done this way, because the presence of music is so universal and inescapable. On a higher level, we may listen for sheer aural pleasure. Our response, if we are listening in this way, is likely to be something like, "That's a pretty song." But there is at least one other way we may listen. We may *actively* participate in the listening experience. We may listen with an intellectual, as well as sensual, attitude of mind. This makes the listener a partner with the composer and performer in a cooperative musical activity, one which is not complete without such participation.

But what does the listener do when he participates actively? What is it that he is listening for? To put it in broad terms, he is listening for musical style. His knowledge of musical elements, and even to a degree his knowledge of form, is most important because it allows him to attend to musical style. An active listener, in attending to style, is making an informal aural stylistic analysis. Of course he is doing this unconsciously. He is allowing his knowledge of style to enhance his musical enjoyment. But before this unconscious act is possible, every listener must first learn to make this informal stylistic analysis in a conscious way. Then, through repeated listening practice, he can make it such a part of himself that it becomes automatic. Only at that point is the highest level of musical enjoyment a real possibility.

In this chapter our goal will be to explore some possible stylistic differences and to establish a routine by which these differences may be discovered as we listen. What differences are possible between styles? Obviously there must be differences in the ways in which musical elements and forms are used. They can be differences in sound, rhythm, melody, texture, harmony, and form. This basic idea can provide the nucleus for a simple approach to stylistic listening.

Taking this as a starting point, let us try to formulate a set of questions which we can ask ourselves about the music as it is being played: questions which, when answered, will provide a profile of the style of the piece.

I. Sound

*

a. What surface features of the sound can be described?

b. What is the instrumentation? What distinctive uses are made of instrumental color?

c. What use is made of dynamics, or loudness levels?

II. Rhythm

*

a. What is the general tempo, or speed?

b. What is the meter?

c. What distinctive rhythmic features can be described?

III. Melody

*

a. What is the range of the melodies used? What is the tessitura, or where does the "middle" of the main melodies lie—high, low, or medium pitch?

b. What is the melodic contour like?

c. What distinctive melodic features can be described?

IV. Texture

*

a. Is the texture thick or thin?

b. How wide is the texture from the highest to the lowest voice?

c. What is the basic texture—monophonic, homophonic, or polyphonic?

d. What distinctive textural features can be described?

V. Harmony

*

a. Is the harmony used more for color or more to advance the motion of the music?

b. Are there distinctive harmonic features that can be described?

VI. Form

*

a. What is the basic form of the piece? Does it use one of the forms we have studied or does it seem to follow some distinctive direction?

b. How are the themes treated? Are they subjected to variation and development? How?

c. What distinctive formal features can be described?

VII. Other Features

*

Are there other distinctive features of the music which have not been considered in categories I-VI?

* * *

As you read this outline, you will undoubtedly notice that the most prominent and pervasive question is that of "distinctive features." This illustrates, in a sense, the nature of style. Most of the questions asked in this analytical routine touch on surface features of the music—features which are descriptive of a particular piece but may not be true differentiators of the style which that piece represents. It is when we consider distinctive features that we touch upon the real essence of a style. Describing these distinctive features is almost always difficult. The more subtle the style, the more difficult the analysis. But it is here that we truly penetrate to the heart of what makes a particular style what it is.

We should now apply this simple routine to actual aural analysis. We turn to two compositions which we have heard earlier in our study: MOZART, *Symphony No. 40* and TCHAIKOVSKY, *Symphony No. 6*. These are very different in style, although similar in form. Our first concern will be to apply our analytical routine to each, and then to draw contrasts.

MOZART: *Symphony No. 40 in G Minor, K.550*

I. Sound

❋

The orchestra is small, consisting of one flute, two oboes, two clarinets, two bassoons, two horns, first and second violins, viola, cello and bass. Cellos and basses play a single bass line. The instruments are used in a straightforward manner and no unusual coloristic devices are employed. There is a variety of dynamics from soft to loud. These dynamics are always one or the other, however; there are no gradual increases or decreases in loudness.

II. Rhythm

❋

The four movements are fast–slow–fast–fast. Movements one and four are in duple meter; movements two and three are triple. There is no employment of mixed meter and no changing of meters within a single movement. Rhythms are simple, and little or no use is made of such rhythmic devices as beat displacement, except in the minuet.

III. Melody

❋

The melodies played by each instrument are kept within a fairly restricted range. No unusual demands are made upon the instruments, so far as range is concerned. A variety of melodic contours are used in the various movements. No generalizations concerning contour are possible. Most of the melodies consist of diatonic, chordal skips and are easily divisible into short motives, which makes development possible.

IV. Texture

*

The texture is fairly wide, from the lowest to the highest voices. It is also usually full, with only very occasional thinning out. The string section is playing most of the time. The basic textural type is homophonic, but within this general texture there is much melodic interest in the individual parts. In other words, there is some polyphony within the basic homophonic texture. Sometimes, this becomes the predominant feature of the texture.

V. Harmony

*

Harmony is used purely to advance the movement of the piece. Although the harmonies are often very interesting, they are not primarily coloristic in use.

VI. Form

*

The symphony is, of course, a typical sonata. The first,

second, and last movements are in sonata-allegro form. The third movement, as is typical of symphonies of this period, is a minuet and trio. The sonata-allegro movements are marked by a relatively simple, but inventive, use of development. The nature of the melodies, being easily divisible into motives, makes this possible. The development is always clear, and the ear can easily detect the source of the thematic material. It amounts mostly to a continuous modulation into a variety of keys, using motive material from the main themes.

VII. Other Distinctive Features

*

No other distinctive features are prominent. In summary, the piece is regular in form, simple in design, inventive in the use of thematic material, balanced and symmetrical in phrase structure, and restrained in harmony and instrumentation.

* * *

TCHAIKOVSKY: *Symphony No. 6 in B Minor, Opus 74*

I. Sound

*

The most obvious thing about this symphony is its large scale. The orchestra is very large: three flutes, piccolo, two oboes, two clarinets, two bassoons, four horns, two trumpets, three trombones, tuba, percussion, first and second violins, viola, cello, and bass. The string parts are often divided, giving, in effect, up to ten lines to the strings alone. The use of instrumental color is great and varied. The wind instruments are prominent, both as individual sections and in combinations between families. Solo parts for wind instruments are frequently employed. Extreme dynamic levels are called for, from the quietest whisper to the loudest levels possible. These dynamic changes often are achieved gradually, with the orchestra making a slow crescendo from soft to loud or a slow diminuendo from loud to soft. The use of dynamics is a major feature of the composition.

II. Rhythm

It is difficult to generalize about the tempi of the four movements. The second and third movements are fast. The first and fourth movements use such a variety of tempi that no generalizations make sense. Meter changes are often found within a single movement. The second movement employs a constant 2+3 mixed meter.

III. Melody

The melodies employed here use the most extreme ranges of the instruments for which they are written, making great demands upon the players. There are two general types of melody employed: vigorous, active ones which are easily divisible into motives and long, flowing, lyric lines of very smooth contour. Melody is one of the most outstanding features of the piece.

IV. Texture

*

The texture is very wide. At times it is thick, with the entire orchestra in action covering a very wide pitch range. At other times the texture is very thin, with only a few instruments playing. The predominant texture is homophonic, but with very great independence of lines within that basic homophony.

V. Harmony

*

The harmony is functional, in that it is used primarily to give motion. But coloristic use is also present. Many full, lush, complex chords are employed. Combined with the colorful instrumentation, this gives the piece its characteristic velvety sound.

VI. Form

*

The formal conception in general is large. Each of the movements is long. The most noticeable formal feature is the very complex use of the sonata-allegro form in the first movement. Each of the themes is really a large theme group, consisting of a wealth of diverse melodic material. In fact, the first theme group contains some developmental material even in the exposition. The second theme contrasts extremely with the first. The lyric and flowing nature of this second theme makes it incapable of undergoing much development. so the development section is based mainly upon the first theme. That development is quite long and contains practically every conceivable device. The form is kept varied by the several changes of tempo within the movement.

VII. Other Distinctive Features

*

We have already pointed out most of the distinctive features audible in the work. The most noticeable stylistic features are the large scale of the piece, colorful harmony and instrumentation, virtuoso use of instruments, lyrical melody, variety of tempi and meters, and variety of dynamics.

* * *

Given these brief analyses, we can now draw some comparative conclusions concerning the styles of the two symphonies. The most revealing way to do this is to address ourselves to the differences between them, since the differences far outweigh any similarities. Let us make a chart illustrating these differences:

MOZART	*	TCHAIKOVSKY
	Sound	
Small orchestra. Little use of instrumental color.		Large orchestra. Great use of instrumental color.
	Rhythm	
Straightforward. No change of meters within movements. No mixed meters.		Many changes of meter and tempi within movements. Use of mixed meter.
	Melody	
Incisive melodies, suitable for development. Limited ranges.		Long, lyrical melodies, less suited for development, alternated with themes more capable of motivic division. Extreme ranges. Chromaticism.
	Texture	
Little variety of texture. Medium textural range.		Variety in thickness and thinness of texture. Wide textural range.

Harmony

Purely functional. Not a great deal of harmonic interest, except as it functions to impart motion and create the sonata form.	Harmony both functional and coloristic. Lush, full chords, Chromatic modulations.

Form

Small forms. Emphasis upon balance and symmetry. Sonata-allegro used in a fashion which is almost "textbook."	Large formal design. Freer use of sonata-allegro.

* * *

This type of analysis could be carried much farther. We are confining ourselves to the most obvious surface aspects of these pieces because these are the ones which are easiest to hear. This process illustrates many of the things which we should listen for and gives us an organized routine for listening. Given some practice in this type of aural analysis, listening skills can be greatly sharpened and musical understanding increased immensely. Given enough practice to make such listening habits automatic and unconscious, enjoyment may be multiplied by a great factor. In order to provide some further practice and to give some glimpse of the vast range of styles which history has given us, we shall, in the next chapter, choose for analysis some typical and significant works of contrasting styles and subject them to the same treatment we have given these two symphonies.

THE ANALYSIS OF STYLE

IN *the previous chapter we devised a routine for stylistic analysis, based upon a set of questions which we may ask about any composition being studied. In this chapter, we shall apply this routine to several pieces of music written in very diverse styles. We have chosen five examples illustrative of five major periods in the history of music: the Baroque, the Classic period, the Romantic period, the Impressionist school, and the Modern period.*

Within any single period many styles may be found; but each period still has its common stylistic features which serve to identify the works with the period. The goal of this chapter is to illustrate further the diversity of musical styles to be found and to provide practice in applying the analytical routine to active listening. Listen to each of the compositions, and make your own analysis before reading the analysis given here. Then compare your analytical comments with the ones printed.

BACH: *Suite No. 3 in D*, Second Movement

I. Sound

The orchestra is small, consisting only of strings and harpsichord. There is little variety of instrumental color.

II. Rhythm

The movement is in a slow, duple meter. The beat is emphasized because the bass instruments and harpsichord play on practically every beat.

III. Melody

The melody is restricted in range and of medium tessitura. The contour is very smooth, consisting of stepwise passages interspaced with wide skips, in such a way that the skips do not diminish the smoothness of the overall melodic shape.

IV. Texture

The texture is not very wide in range and is neither particularly thick or thin. It consists of two interlocking polyphonic voices over a persistent background of bass and harpsichord.

V. Harmony

The harmonic structure is purely functional: it is used solely to induce motion. Harmonic color plays little or no part.

VI. Form

The form is sectional, being basically an expanded binary form. The chief thematic device is repetition, there being little variation and no motivic development.

VII. Distinctive Features and Stylistic Summary

The piece is characterized by restricted ranges, paucity of instrumental color, polyphonic texture, and the use of the continuous bass and harpsichord foundation, known as "basso continuo."

* * *

These are all features which characterize most of the music from the Baroque period. But we must distinguish between features characterizing a single piece and those common to an entire period. Every point in the above analysis is useful as a guide for listening, but not all are characteristic of Baroque music in general. The lack of variation and development might lead to the conclusion that such techniques were not important in the Baroque. This is not true. Generalizations can be made only on the basis of large numbers of works analyzed. What we are doing here is simply illustrating stylistic diversity and providing listening practice.

HAYDN: *Symphony No. 101, Clock*, First Movement

I. Sound

The instrumentation consists of strings and some winds. The orchestra is small, with relatively minor use of instrumental color. There are many changes in dynamics, all of which occur suddenly.

II. Rhythm

The movement begins with a slow introduction, followed by the movement proper in fast duple meter. The rhythm is characterized by occasional accents on normally weak beats.

III. Melody

The melodies cover a fairly wide range, with medium tessitura. Stepwise and skipwise motion are present in about even proportions. Contours are more varied and complex than in the previous example.

IV. Texture

The texture is wider in range and somewhat thicker than the last example. There is little textural variety. The basic type is homophonic, but with much melodic interest in practically all the voice parts.

V. Harmony

The harmony is entirely functional, harmonic color being of little importance. The progressions are very straightforward and "normal." There are few harmonic surprises anywhere in the movement.

VI. Form

The form is strict sonata-allergro. All the points character-istics of this form are observed. There is a great deal of motivic development in the middle section, employing a variety of developmental techniques. Form is obviously of major importance.

VII. Distinctive Features and Stylistic Summary

Straightforward harmony, emphasis upon form, and the limited use of orchestral color characterize the music. Also important are the sudden dynamic changes and the clever use of development.

* * *

TCHAIKOVSKY: *Violin Concerto in D*, First Movement

I. Sound

The most noticeable first impression of this piece is the lush sound. The orchestra is very large, with a great variety of instrumentation. Instrumental color is much in evidence, and the use of winds instruments is far greater than in the previous example. There are many changes of dynamics, and they are not all sudden, as in the Haydn symphony. There are many gradual increases and decreases in loudness.

II. Rhythm

The tempo is medium slow and the meter is duple. There is no particularly prominent rhythmic usage.

III. Melody

The range is very wide, with medium tessitura. The contours are varied and complex. The melody lines are very long and sustained.

IV. Texture

The texture is very wide in range and fairly thick. The movement is basically monophonic, but there are many points of imitation between the orchestra and the solo violin, and much melodic interest in the subordinate voices.

V. Harmony

The harmony is basically functional, but there is a considerable coloristic use of harmony, as well. This is as a result of many seventh chords and chromatically altered chords.

VI. Form

The movement is basically sonata-allegro. This is a much freer use of the form, however, than heard in the previous example. There is a great use of modulation. There is some variation, but not such a great use of motivic development. There is more repetition than in the Haydn movement.

VII. Distinctive Features and Stylistic Summary

The movement is marked by the large orchestra, the use of instrumental color, long and lush melodies, colorful harmony, and the very free use of the basic form employed.

* * *

RESPIGHI: *Pines of Rome*, The Villa Borghese

I. Sound

Here is a profound stylistic difference from the previous examples. The orchestra is large, with great use of instrumental color. For the first time we hear solo instruments used as part of the orchestral texture. We also hear the mute used for the first time on a wind instrument (trumpet). There is a very wide dynamic range, including both sudden and gradual increases and decreases of loudness. The basic sound is very brilliant and arresting.

II. Rhythm

The tempo is fast. The basic meter is duple, but very difficult to follow at times. There are several shifts of accent. The overall character is one of great vigor.

III. Melody

The contours are quite jagged. There is a predominance of high tessitura and wide ranges. The melodic structure is very complex, producing an arresting melody but one which is hardly singable.

IV. Texture

The texture is extremely wide and thick. It is basically homophonic, but there is much interesting and complex melodic movement in all the voices.

V. Harmony

The harmony is marked by acrid dissonances and unusual progressions. While still functional, the most noticeable use of harmony is for color.

VI. Form

The formal design is very free, following no set or conventional pattern. There is considerable use of repetition, some variation, but little of what we know as motivic development. The basic design is one of free arrangement of sections, each one flowing smoothly into the next.

VII. Distinctive Features and Stylistic Summary

This piece may be said to use everything in excess, but always for an artistic purpose. Color is the key word. Harmony, melody, and instrumentation all point in that direction. While maintaining a coherent form, the emphasis is upon the sensuous impact of the sound.

* * *

STRAVINSKY: *Petrouchka*, Tableau 1

I. Sound

The immediate effect is one of great color. The orchestra is large, with a variety of instrumental treatment. Dynamic levels are many and varied, as in the Respighi example.

II. Rhythm

The tempo is quite fast. The meter is highly irregular, and the entire piece is marked by rapidly shifting accents, so much so in fact that the meter cannot be readily determined by the ear.

III. Melody

The melodies are of two distinct types: catchy, folklike tunes alternating with more difficult, strictly instrumental-style sections. These instrumental melodies are mostly of very jagged contour.

IV. Texture

The texture is very wide. It varies from extremely thick to thin. The monophonic structure contains a very high degree of interest in the lower and inner voices as well as the main melodies. The shift from thick to thin is frequently done quite suddenly.

V. Harmony

The harmonies are frequently acrid and colorful, but the harmony is mainly functional, much more so than in the Respighi example. There is extensive use of polytonality—more than one tonal center at a time.

VI. Form

The form is sectional, with a considerable use of repetition. The treatment is quite free. Some slight amount of variation is used, but very little motivic development. In effect, the melodies are constantly being subjected to minor changes, almost from measure to measure.

VII. Distinctive Features and Stylistic Summary

The main features of this piece are the unique rhythmic treatment, polytonality, and the use of folk melodies interspersed with more complex themes. Of note also is the imaginative use of instruments, including use of extreme ranges.

* * *

By this time, you should be acquiring more facility in applying an analytical routine to active listening. It should be emphasized that in this exercise we have come to the reason for this book's existence: to assist you in becoming an active and intelligent listener, equipped with the knowledge and skill necessary to become an active participant in the musical experience. As you listen on your own initiative in the future, this act should become so easy as to be unconscious. It is at that time that your musical knowledge and practice will fullfill its goal—that of becoming an indispensable aid to musical enjoyment.

CONTEMPORARY AND NON-WESTERN MUSIC

IN *the preceding chapters we have seen how music is constructed. We have analyzed its structure from its most basic elements through its more complex forms and have seen how this structure serves artistic purposes. But, as we have pointed out previously, we have been studying only one musical system which is employed in most of the music to which we are accustomed. Nevertheless, much music exists in which few features of this system play a part.*

The existence of such music, exemplified by music of other cultures and by much contemporary Western music, poses some significant aesthetic questions and places different demands upon the listener. In this chapter we shall look at a few examples of some of these differences, just in order to become aware of their existence. Before doing so, however, it will be helpful to summarize the most important features of the Western musical system which we have studied thus far. Conceptually, we may divide music into three groups of elements: tonal, rhythmic, and formal.

The formal aspects of Western music have grown from the requirements and the possibilities contained within the tonal and rhythmic elements. For the most part, the forms have been based upon a juxtaposition, interaction, and metamorphosis of themes. By themes we mean identifiable material made up of tonal and rhythmic elements—chiefly melody. It is only a slight exaggeration to say that comprehension of musical form is primarily the recognition of melodic material.

Just as traditional Western music can be divided into tonal, rhythmic, and formal elements, so can all other musical systems. But these elements are to be found in different guises in other systems. In fact, some of them are so different from their counterparts in our familiar music that one could question whether they are even properly placed in the same categories. Let us illustrate the point by considering the way these elements appear in some other musical systems.

Twelve-Tone and Serial Music

*

At the end of the nineteenth century, many composers had employed modulation to a degree which obscured and seemed to exhaust the possible uses of tonality. In response to this, some composers began to search for new ways to organize their music. An extreme position was that of the atonalists, who thought that tonality should be abandoned entirely and music should be written in such a way that no key center was implied. Twelve-tone music and serial composition grew out of that position.

Twelve-tone composition, although complex in practice, is easy to understand in theory. It begins with the notion that each of the twelve tones of the chromatic scale is equal to each of the others. In order to insure this equality, certain principles of composition were established.

Each piece was to be based upon a tone row, or series, containing all twelve tones of the chromatic scale arranged in some order decided upon by the composer. The tones were then to be used in that order, with no tone being repeated until the other eleven had been used either melodically or harmonically. This use of a "series" gave the technique its name: serial composition.

If the composer were restricted to just this one row for his composition, he would be greatly hampered. So several forms of the row are allowed: the row itself, the inversion of the row, the retrograde, and the retrograde inversion. In addition, each of these four forms may be transposed to begin on any pitch of the twelve available in the chromatic scale. This gives a total of forty-eight versions of each row.

Twelve-tone composition seemed at first to be suitable only for short works. But as the technique evolved, it became apparent that longer compositions could be written using the new technique. An example of such a work is:

SCHOENBERG: *Woodwind Quintet, Opus 26*

As serial composition became more common, several important variations appeared. For one, the idea of the series was applied to rows of fewer than twelve tones. The principles, however, remained the same. A famous example is:

STRAVINSKY: *In Memoriam, Dylan Thomas*

The explicitness—some would mistakenly say rigidity—of the principles of serial composition seemed to give the composer much greater control over his tonal materials. For artists who were inclined to value this control, serial composition held great promise. Some got the idea of serializing not just the pitches upon which the piece would be based, but also of serializing the other aspects of the music: rhythm, dynamics, timbre—everything which the composition comprised.

Here is an example of total serialization:

BOULEZ: *Piano Sonata No. 2*

This raises many questions of a practical nature, and some philosophical ones as well. How can this music be understood by the ear, since it is so complex and contains little for which we are trained to listen? Is control of artistic material more important than presenting to the listener some easily understood expressive content? With such control over the material exercised by the composer, what is the role of the performer, and is this role minimized? These are questions of great importance to serious composition in the twentieth century.

Electronic Music

*

This is a category which includes many different kinds of music, produced in a variety of ways. It had its roots in the growing desire of composers to exercise greater control over their material. The technological advances in producing electronic sound and in electronic recording equipment made during the past several decades have made this possible. The one thing which all electronic music shares in common is the fact that it is recorded directly upon magnetic tape and does not require the services of a performer to bring it to life. This is true even though some music has been written for electronic tape *plus* live performers.

Perhaps the earliest attempt at tape music was known as *musique concrète.* This employed tape recorded sounds usually considered to be non-musical. Once recorded, the sounds (bird calls, thunder, falling rocks, automobile traffic—anything) could be combined and re-recorded in any way the composer wished. They could be transformed by speeding up or slowing down the tape, they could be played backward, or their timbre could be changed by playing them through electronic filter circuits. This variety of material could be put together in such a way as to produce a recognizable form.

From this beginning it was a short step to the so-called classical tape studio. The recording techniques employed by the classical tape composer were similar to those of the producer of *musique concrète,* but with a major difference. The classical studio contains equipment designed to produce sound of a specified pitch and wave form. The composer, rather than relying upon whatever sounds he can find, is allowed to produce sounds over which he has more control, sounds which are musical to begin with. From that point on he can combine and transform these sounds into whatever musical form he wishes, using the same tape and filtering techniques worked out by composers of *musique concrète.*

It was with the classical studio that electronic music first began to come into its own. But the techniques associated with this method of composition are very slow. Each musical tone has be be generated separately. Compositions are put together by painstaking cutting and editing, filtering and re-recording. This led musicians and engineers to seek some way to add flexibility and shorten the time required to produce a given amount of music. The result is the electronic music synthesizer, which provides sound generating equipment, control circuits, filtering and sound-altering units, and mixing circuits in one instrument. The synthesizer also provides a flexible means of control which greatly increases the range of possibilities open to the composer, while at the same time reducing the amount of drudge work required. Although tape composition still requires cutting, splicing, and re-recording, this requirement has been greatly minimized. It is fair to say that, at this time, the synthesizer occupies the most prominent position in electronic music, although other techniques are still used.

Before going further, let us hear some examples of electronic music. The following are examples of classical tape music and synthesizer music, respectively.

VARESE: *Poeme Electronique*

SUBOTNICK: *Silver Apples of the Moon*

One interesting feature of electronic music is its lack of dependence upon notation. Since the music is recorded directly on tape and no performer is required, no notation is necessary in order to communicate to that performer. Sometimes scores are made, for study purposes, after an electronic piece is recorded. In some instances a composer may notate a composition for his own guidance in making the actual tape. The type of notation used for such music bears little resemblance to standard musical notation. As an example of one type of notation employed for electronic music, Example 15.1 shows the score for a part of *Silver Apples of the Moon.*

Some notes on Silver Apples of the Moon:

"A single silver child-angel in a glittering garden of silver star-fruit"

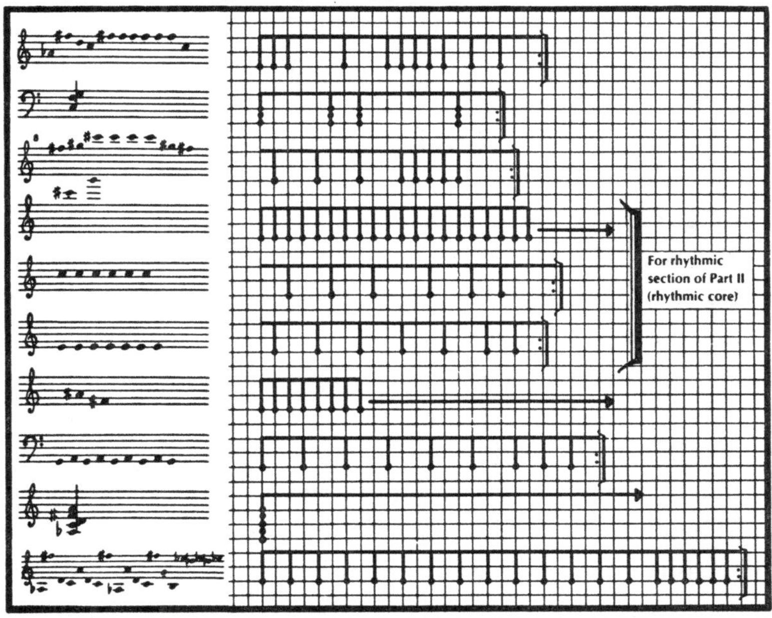

Ex. 15.1

Computer Controlled Music

*

Perhaps the most ambitious attempt at complete control of materials by electronic means is to be found in computer music. It is important not to confuse this with music which is written by a computer but intended for performance by conventional instruments. The computer music of which we speak uses the computer only to produce the sounds. The composer codes his music for input into the computer in such a way that he specifies for the machine the wave forms which he wants produced. This is done by a complex mathematical process which requires hours of computer time to produce minutes of music. The computer then translates the data given it by the composer into instructions for a machine called a digital-to-analog converter which, in turn, produces a series of voltages according to the computer's instructions. These voltages are fed directly into a tape recorder which produces the composition in complete and final form. This involves no cutting, splicing, or any of the other techniques associated with classical and synthesizer music. It gives the composer absolute control over every aspect of his piece, making possible the production of music which would be impossible, in many instances, for human players to perform. It also results in a very expensive piece of music, because of the computer time required. For this reason, little of this kind of music has been written.

Aleatoric Music

*

The aesthetic principle involved in total serialization and in much electronic music is that of increased control of the music by the composer. In such music the performer, where employed at all, is expected simply to reproduce, in as exact a way as possible, the creation of the composer. A very different point of view is embodied in *aleatoric* music, often referred to as chance music. The term chance music is, in many respects, a misnomer. Aleatoric music is not entirely dependent upon chance, but rather employs some elements of chance or probability in its realization. This is done in a bewildering variety of ways.

An example is found in Example 15.2. This is the first page of the score to *And Come Up Dripping* by David Rosenboom. This piece is for oboe reed and electronic sound which is altered and combined with the live performance. In playing the music scored in the illustration, the performer may begin with any of the oblong boxes. The other markings are directions for the electronic system operator. The small markings inside the circle indicate switching of the time delay devices in the four-channel system. The symbols in the outer circle indicate kinds of sound treatment (f) and rate of electronic repetition (r). The reed player is instructed to "play all the material in one box until he feels the material is exhausted" and then move on to the next box.

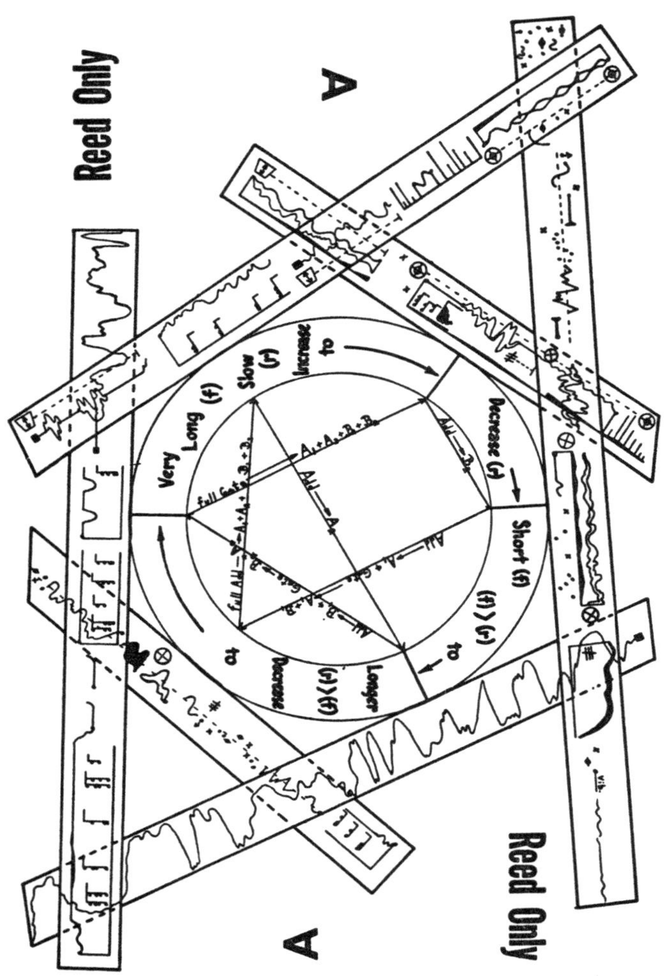
Reed Only
A
Very Long (f)
Slow (r)
Increase to
Decrease (r)
Short (f)
(f) > (r) to
Longer (r) < (f)
Decrease to
Reed Only
A

Ex. 15.2

This illustrates one way in which chance may be employed in the creation of a musical composition. There is no end to the number of ways which might be devised. Each piece presents its own possibilities and, incidentally, requires its own notational system. In a real sense, aleatoric music cannot be recorded. Once a piece is put on tape or record, it is fixed; and aleatoric music depends upon spontaneity and chance. In actual practice, an aleatoric composition is different each time it is performed, and is therefore not subject to being "frozen" by recording. A recording can only present one actual realization from an infinite universe of possible interpretations.

Non-Western Music

*

The music which we have been discussing in this chapter is, of course, very different from that music to which we have become accustomed in our everyday lives. It employs technical and aesthetic differences that, in a sense, belong to a different musical culture. The familiar elements of melody, harmony, texture, timbre, rhythm, and form are employed quite differently. The same challenges occur for the listener in the case of much music from other parts of the world. A few brief examples will illustrate this.

Central and East African music may serve to illustrate a very different treatment of rhythm. Here are polyrhythms so complex that they defy our system of notation and pose great challenges to Western performers. It is nearly impossible for a Western listener to tell what is going on in this music by hearing it. Its rhythmic complexity and sublety are too great. When one is confronted with this music, it illustrates a fact about most of our own music: ours is rhythmically simple, even in its most highly developed manifestations.

A different treatment of tonal elements may be found in the music of the Middle East and the Far East. Much of the music of the Middle East divides the octave into many more divisions than the twelve to which we are accustomed. This means that the tones are much closer together than they are in our tonal system, thus allowing for greater subtlety of melody. This is largely lost to our ears, because we are not accustomed to such small intervals. The melodic subtlety and microtonal division of the octave serve to make harmony difficult, so this music is usually restricted to one line.

Many of the cultures of the Far East employ scales of fewer tones than ours, predominantly five-tone, or pentatonic, scales. This may result in rather restricted and somewhat static melodies because of the absence of half-steps.

A different treatment of form is illustrated by the music of India. The forms of Indian music stem directly from the construction of a complicated system of tonal relationships known as *ragas*. Each raga is constructed according to principles well known to Indian musicians, but sometimes seeming rather obscure to Western listeners. Here are some recorded examples of Non-Western music:

Africa—East and West:	Institute of Ethnomusicology, Record 1 ER6751
Music of India:	Baerenreiter Musicaphon, 4 volumes, BM 30L 2006, 2007, 2018, 2021
Music of Japan:	Baerenreiter Musicaphon, 6 volumes, BM 30C 2012–2017
Arabic and Druse Music:	Folkways Records, FE 4480
Japanese Folk Music:	Lyrichord, LLST 7163
Ragas and Talas:	World Pacific Records, WP 1431

Implications for the Listener

*

The discussions thus far in this chapter have been for one purpose: to help the reader become aware of the existence of many musical systems. The existence of many systems raises questions and poses problems for the listener.

Perhaps the most important implication of this state of affairs has to do with culture and its part in defining expectations for the listener. There is no doubt that each culture conditions its members to its particular elements. This includes art and music. To our ears, the music of the Middle East may sound chaotic and strange. But to a member of a Mid-East culture, the music has meaning. It is very difficult to cast aside our own conditioning and listen to such music with the ears of a person belonging to another culture. Still, this is what we must attempt to do if we are to begin to understand music other than our own. This is just as true in the case of much contemporary Western music as it is of non-Western music. For, in a sense, this music belongs to a culture different from that which produced the music of the eighteenth and nineteenth centuries and also from that which produces modern popular music.

Another important question raised is that of the relative importance of composer and performer. Traditionally, the two have had a kind of partnership in creating the musical experience. With the advent of the total control made possible by serialization and electronic music, the importance of the performer is minimized. With aleatoric music, the reverse is true: the composer has effaced himself somewhat in favor of the performer. This raises a secondary question. Must art necessarily involve a consciously devised order, or can artistic meaning be imputed to accidental, disorderly, or constantly changing forms? This is a question which will probably be debated centuries from now just as it has been for centuries past. Nevertheless, it is a fundamental and very important question.

Finally, we come to the question of defining music and its elements. Must music be composed of melody, rhythm, and harmony as usually defined? If so, much modern music does not qualify. This music requires a complete redefinition of musical elements and forms and a reformulation of many basic aesthetic questions.

These are questions which have no definitive answers. However, the implications for the listener are clear. The listener must adopt a posture suited to each piece; he cannot adopt a rigid attitude and expect to get much from the more esoteric works. The rewards for displaying this flexibility are great, even if the task is diffficult.

Our discussions and analyses have now come to an end. They have been necessarily brief and rudimentary. But, after all, our aim has been simply to introduce the main techniques and forms of Western music. We have done this and have met along the way some of the landmarks of this musical tradition. We have done this with one goal in mind: to help unlock some of the meaning and pleasure available in music.

The real value is in the music itself.

Enjoy it!

Bibliography

The following list is intended for those who wish to read further. It is not to be considered a complete or exhaustive bibliography. For those whose reading time is limited, but who wish to pursue the subject of musical structure and style somewhat farther than this book has made possible, The Art of Music *by Cannon, Johnson, and Waite and* The Sense of Music *by Zuckerkandl are especially recommended.*

BIBLIOGRAPHY

Cannon, Beekman C., Johnson, Alvin H., and Waite, William G.
The Art of Music New York: The Thomas Y. Crowell Co. (1960)

Cope, David
New Directions in Music Dubuque, Iowa: William C. Brown Co. (1971)

Grout, Donald Jay
A History of Western Music New York: W. W. Norton (1973)

LaRue, Jan
Guidelines for Style Analysis New York: W. W. Norton (1970)

Machlis, Joseph
Introduction to Contemporary Music New York: W. W. Norton (1961)

Peyser, Joan
The New Music New York: Dell Publishing Co. Inc. (1971)

Piston, Walter
Harmony New York: W. W. Norton (1941)

Trythall, Gilbert
Principles and Practice of Electronic Music New York: Grosset and Dunlap Inc. (1973)

White, John D.
Music in Western Culture: A Short History Dubuque, Iowa: William C. Brown Co. (1972)

Zuckerkandl, Victor
The Sense of Music Princeton, New Jersey: Princeton University Press (1959)

Chronology

An
alphabetical list
of composers,
together with life dates
and countries of birth,
of all
recorded examples
cited.

Bach, Johann Sebastian	1685-1750	Germany
Barber, Samuel	1910-	USA
Bartók, Bela	1881-1945	Hungary
Beethoven, Ludwig van	1770-1827	Germany
Berkeley, Lennox	1903-	England
Berlioz, Hector	1803-1869	France
Borodin, Alexander	1834-1887	Russia
Boulez, Pierre	1925-	France
Brahms, Johannes	1833-1897	Germany
Britten, Benjamin	1913-	England
Byrd, William	1543-1623	England
Chavez, Carlos	1899-	Mexico
Chopin, Frederic	1810-1849	Poland
Copland, Aaron	1900-	USA
Couperin, Francois	1668-1733	France
Creston, Paul	1906-	USA
Debussy, Claude	1862-1918	France
Elgar, Edward	1857-1934	England
Franck, César	1822-1890	Belgium
Gabrieli, Giovanni	1557-1612	Italy
Hahn, Reynaldo	1874-1946	France
Haydn, Franz Joseph	1732-1809	Austria
Hindemith, Paul	1895-1963	Germany
Holst, Gustav	1874-1934	England

Ibert, Jacques	1890-1962	France
Ives, Charles	1874-1954	USA
Kodàly, Zoltan	1882-1967	Hungary
Mozart, Wolfgang Amadeus	1756-1791	Austria
Mussorgsky, Modest	1839-1881	Russia
Palestrina, Giovanni Pierluigi	1525-1594	Italy
Puccinni, Giacomo	1858-1924	Italy
Purcell, Henry	1659-1695	England
Ravel, Maurice	1875-1937	France
Respighi, Ottorino	1879-1936	Italy
Rodrigo, Joachim	1902-	Spain
Scarlatti, Domenico	1685-1757	Italy
Schoenberg, Arnold	1874-1951	Austria
Schubert, Franz	1797-1828	Austria
Schumann, Robert	1810-1856	Germany
Sousa, John Phillip	1856-1932	USA
Strauss, Richard	1864-1949	Germany
Stravinsky, Igor	1882-1971	Russia
Subotnick, Morton	1933-	USA
Tchaikovsky, Peter	1840-1893	Russia
Varèse, Edgard	1885-1965	France
Vaughan Williams, Ralph	1872-1958	England
Wagner, Richard	1813-1883	Germany
Webern, Anton von	1883-1945	Austria

Listed below are all recorded examples cited in the text. Most of these are readily available in music libraries and record stores. For those compositions which might be more difficult to find, a source is given. In the case of a composition which has been recorded more than once, a single source is given in order to simplify the listing. This is not necessarily the performance which is considered to be the best, but is a typical performance of the composition in question.

BACH:

The Art of Fugue 88, 89

Brandenburg Concerto No. 2 84

Brandenburg Concerto No. 3 19, 76

Brandenburg Concerto No. 5 155

Brandenburg Concerto No. 6 75

Ich habe genug 186

"Little" Fugue in G Minor 142

Passacaglia in C Minor 141

Suite No. 3 in C for Cello 44

Suite No. 3 in D for Orchestra 89, 207

Wachet Auf 32, 186

BARBER:

Adagio for Strings 23

BARTÓK:

Quartet No. 1 43

BEETHOVEN:

Octet in E-flat for Winds, Opus 103 43
(London 6442)

Piano Concerto No. 4 in G, Opus 58 153

Quartet No. 1, Opus 18, No. 1 153

Quartet No. 14, Opus 131 81

Sonata Pathètique in C Minor, Opus 13 135, 149

Sonata in G, Opus 14, No. 2 120, 138

Sonata No. 9, Opus 47, Violin and Piano 44

Symphony No. 3, Opus 55 38, 77, 126

Symphony No. 5, Opus 67 109

Symphony No. 6, Opus 68 40

Symphony No. 8, Opus 93 75, 84

BERKELEY:

Sonatina for Guitar, Opus 51 44

(Antiqua AN 1003)

BERLIOZ:

Requiem 45

BORODIN:

Quartet No. 2 in D 43

(London STS 15046)

BOULEZ:

Piano Sonata No. 2 222

(Finnadar 9004)

BRAHMS:

Capriccio, Opus 76, No. 5 61

(Mercury MA 15024)

Intermezzo, Opus 76, No. 3 59

(Mercury MA 15024)

Liebeslieder Waltzes, Opus 52 and Opus 65 45

Piano Concerto No. 1 in D Minor, Opus 15 153

Quartet No. 1, Opus 51, No. 1 43

Symphony No. 3, Opus 90 62

Variations on a Theme of Haydn, Opus 56a 123

BRITTEN:

Variations on a Theme of Purcell 23

(Columbia S 31808)

BYRD:

Pavana: The Earl of Salisbury 33

(Archive ARC 73201)

CARLOS:
Switched-On Bach 34
(Columbia MS 7194)
CHAVEZ:
Sinfonia India 54
CHOPIN:
Fantasy in F Minor, Opus 49 44
COPLAND:
El Salon Mexico 29, 60
"Simple Gifts" from Old American Songs 174
(Oiseau Lyre OL 50145)
COUPERIN:
Les Nonètes 131
(Vox SVBX 5448)
CRESTON:
Sonata for Saxophone and Piano, Opus 19 31
(Golden Crest 7037)
DEBUSSY:
La Cathédrale engloutie 102
(Vox SVBX 5433)
La Chevelure 174
(London 26043)
Cloches à travers les feuilles 77
(Columbia MS 6567)
Golliwog's Cakewalk 59
(Columbia MS 6567)
Pagodes 77
(Angel S 36874)

Reflets dans l'eau 102
(Vox SVBX 5433)
Syrinx 44
(Orion 6911)

ELGAR:
Enigma Variations, Opus 36 123
(Angel S 36120)

ETHNIC MUSIC:
Various recorded examples 231

FRANCK:
Symphony in D Minor 31

GABRIELI:
Sonata Pian' e Forte 43
(Archive ARC 3154)

HAHN:
L'Heure Exquise 171
(Victor LCT 1133)

HANDEL:
Messiah 84, 86, 185
Suite No. 1 in B-flat 156
(Columbia M 31512)

HAYDN:
Symphony No. 101, Clock 209

HINDEMITH:
Kleine Kammermusik, Opus 24, No. 2 43
(Mace S 9053)
Morgenmusik for Brass 19, 27
(Crystal S 102)

Frauenliebe und Leben 175
From Foreign Lands 134
(Columbia MS 6411)
Jasminenstrauch 174
(Deutsche Grammophon 139326)
Soldiers' March 133
(Telefunken 25082-25085)
Träumerei 134
(Columbia MS 6411)

SOUSA:
El Capitan 42
(Everest SDBR 3260)

STRAUSS:
Also sprach Zarathustra, Opus 30 20, 81
Tod und Verklärung 159

STRAVINSKY:
In Memoriam, Dylan Thomas 221
Histoire du Soldat 43
Petrouchka 38, 214

SUBOTNICK:
Silver Apples of the Moon 34, 224
(Nonesuch 71174)

TCHAIKOVSKY:
Nutcracker Suite, The Sugar Plum Fairy 30
Romeo and Juliet 158
Symphony No. 6 in B Minor, Opus 74 38, 53, 198
Violin Concerto in D, Opus 35 153, 211

Index

INDEX

INDEX

1 2 3 4 5 6 7 8 9—RJC—82 81 80 79 78 77 76 75 74